DIANE VON FURSTENBERG

OWN IT

THE SECRET TO LIFE

8

AWARE. ALIVE. AWAKE.
AWARENESS
ALONE
AUTHENTICITY
ALLURE
AGE
ABUNDANCE
AUTUMN
ATTENTION
ADVENTURE
ADVOCACY
AROMA
ASSUMER
ATTITUDE
AFFIRMATION
ANGER
ADDICTION
APPRECIATE

22

CHARACTER
CLARITY
CONNECT
COMPASSION
CEREMONY
COMMUNITY
COMMUNICATION
CREATIVITY
COHERENCE
COURAGE
COMMITMENT
CURRENCY
COMPLAIN
COMPASS
CONFIDENCE
CLOUD
COOL
CHILDREN

40

ENERGY
EMPATHY
ENLIGHTENMENT
ESTEEM
EXPAND
EVOLUTION
ESSENCE
EXISTENCE
EGO
ENVY
ENEMY
EX
EFFORTLESS

46

FREEDOM
FAME
FAKE
FEMALE
FAMILY
FIRE
FASHION
FORGIVE
FEELING
FEET
FORTUNE
FEAR
FUTURE
FRIENDS
FRAGILITY

16

BLUE
BLISS
BEAUTY
BLACK & WHITE
BEGINNING
BIRTH
BEING
BELONGING
BED
BATH
BLOOD
BIRTHDAY
BODY
BLAME

30

DIGNITY
DEATH
DAILY PRACTICES
DESTINY
DAWN
DIARY
DYNASTY
DISCOVERY
DIALOGUE
DIET
DISCIPLINE
DOORS
DARKNESS
DAUGHTER
DATA
DRESS
DENIAL
DARE
DOUBT
DREAM

54

GREEN
GRATITUDE
GENEROSITY
GOD

GOOD
GARDEN
GLAMOUR
GREED
GEO (-GRAPHY,
-LOGY, -METRY)
GIFT

60

HAPPINESS
HARMONY
HEART
HEALING
HEALTH
HOME
HUMILITY
HISTORY
HABITS
HORIZON
HAIR
HUMANITY

68

IN CHARGE
INSPIRATION
INTELLIGENCE
INDEPENDENCE
INFINITY
IMMORTALITY
INTIMACY
INTUITION
INTEGRATION
IMAGE
INSECURITY
INTENSITY
INTENTION
INVISIBLE
IRRESISTIBLE
ICON
IMPOSTOR

76

JOY
JUSTICE
JOURNEY
JEALOUSY

80

KNOWLEDGE
KEY
KINDNESS
KISMET

84

LOVE
LIFE
LIVING
LIES
LIGHT
LUCK
LAUGHTER
LEADERSHIP
LEGEND
LOSER
LEGACY
LIBERATED
LOYALTY
LUXURY

90

MOTHER
MIND
MYSTERY
MENTOR

MAGIC
MISUNDERSTANDING
MEMORIES
MIRROR

96

NARCISSISM
NATURE
NUANCE
NO

100

OWN IT
ORANGE
ORACLE
OPINION
OBSESSION
OBSTACLE
ORIGINAL
OFFLINE
OASIS

106

PURPOSE
PLEASURE
PINK
PURPLE
PRESENT
POWER
PROGRESS
PASSION
PEACE
PRACTICE
PROVOCATIVE
PACKING
PICTURE

PILLARS
PROTECTION
PROVENANCE
PAST
POPULARITY
PERSEVERANCE
POINT OF VIEW
PERSONALITY

114

QUESTION
QUALITY TIME
QUIET
QUOTE

118

RED
RITUALS
RELEVANT
RELATIONSHIP
RESPONSIBILITY
REFLECTION
REGROUP
ROUTINE
REGRET
RESTRICTIONS

124

SERENITY
SILENCE
SOLITUDE
SENSITIVITY
SHAME
SUTRAS
SUCCESS
STILLNESS

SPACE
SOUL
SURVIVAL
STRENGTH
SHARING
SUMMER
SEX
STRATEGY
SUNSET
SOUVENIR
SIMPLICITY
SHADOW
SUBSTANCE
SERENDIPITY

132

TRUTH
TRUST
TABLE
TIME
TRANSPARENT

138

UNIVERSE
UNION
UNITY

142

VISIONARY
VOYAGE
VICTORY
VULNERABILITY
VOCATION
VOICE
VICTIM

148

WHITE
WORDS
WORK
WINTER
WATER
WILLPOWER
WOMAN
WINK
WHY ME?

154

X FACTOR

158

YOU/YOURSELF
YELLOW
YES

162

ZEBRA
ZIGZAG
ZEN

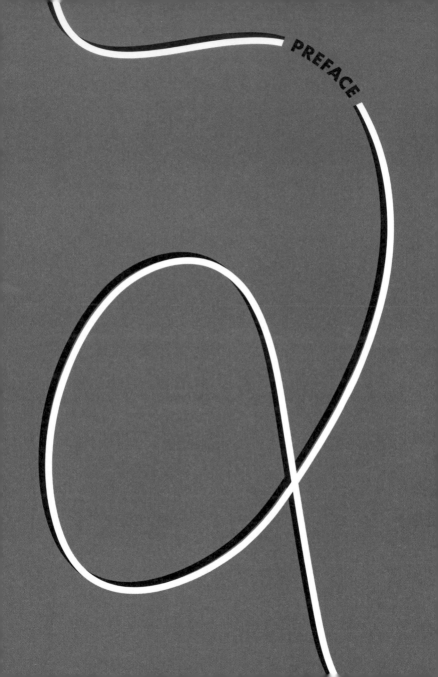

PREFACE

Words have power. We must use them carefully. They create energy, define us, impact our lives and the paths we take. My mother was strict about using the right words, and she loved to use and create aphorisms—a habit I inherited.

When I was first approached by my editor to do a book on these "fragments of truth," I immediately accepted. Sharing my experiences, knowledge, and wisdom is my favorite thing to do. At my age it is allowed and hopefully inspiring!

To achieve this task, I picked words that speak to me most and reflected on their meanings. To put order into my thought process, I decided to organize them as a little dictionary. It was going to be a fun and light exercise on the verge of being frivolous.

But as I was in the midst of writing, the COVID-19 pandemic happened, and with it, home confinement and a new reality. All of a sudden, every word, every sentence took on a whole other dimension, and everything became deeper, more meaningful.

Like everyone else, confinement forced me to pause and made me reevaluate who I was and what mattered most. Whether personally or in my business, I had to confront what was not right anymore and accept what had to change. I had to face all the difficulties I was encountering and own them.

To OWN IT is to accept the truth and deal with it, however unpleasant it may be. It is about being InCharge. It is the secret to life. To be InCharge is not an aggressive statement. It is first and foremost a commitment to ourselves. It is accepting and standing for who we are. We own our imperfections, they become our assets; we own our vulnerability, it becomes our strength. To be InCharge is the core of our power. It is the shelter we carry, the home inside ourselves. Once we achieve that, we are able to connect, expand, inspire, and advocate.

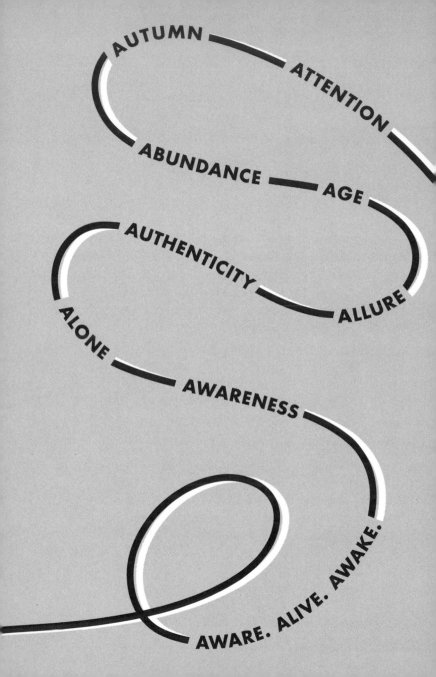

AUTUMN — ATTENTION — ABUNDANCE — AGE — AUTHENTICITY — ALLURE — ALONE — AWARENESS — AWARE. ALIVE. AWAKE.

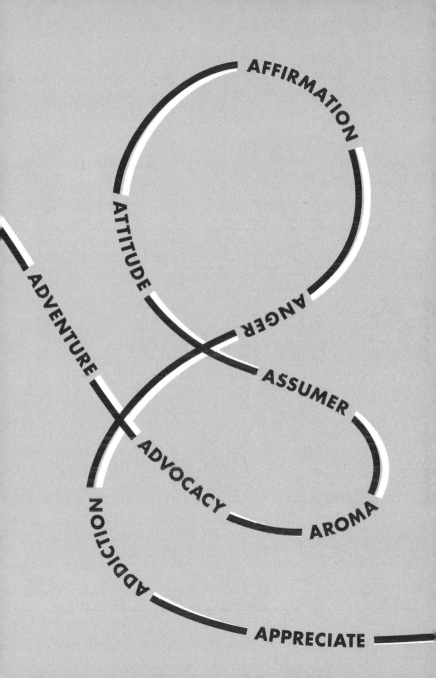

AWARE. ALIVE. AWAKE.

All three words embody OWN IT.

AWARENESS

Awareness is full presence and consciousness. It is knowing who we are, where we are, and noticing everything around us. It is seeing, hearing, feeling. Awareness is assessing the gratitude of being alive. It is making an accurate, honest assessment of where we are in our journey.

As a young girl, I wanted to show that I was strong, so I did not smile much and acted tough. Later I discovered that showing my vulnerability does NOT reveal weakness, and that a joyous laugh and a smile can show strength too. As I became more aware, I felt more comfortable sharing who I was.

ALONE

Being alone is NOT being lonely. It is being whole . . . it is where we find our strength and our full potential. Being alone is the best way to reboot. *See* SOLITUDE.

AUTHENTICITY

Nothing is more attractive and powerful than authenticity. It is the essence of who we really are and so much better than any imitation. *See* ORIGINAL.

ALLURE

Allure is the mysterious aura that happens when our external image matches our inner being. To have allure comes naturally with self-awareness, acceptance, and the independent spirit of *owning it*.

AGE

Age is the map of life . . . made of memories, stored images, emotions, and experiences. Aging needs to be celebrated every moment, every day, every year. Age is the proof of having lived.

Living and loving our age is OWNING IT!

ABUNDANCE

Although abundance is rewarding, it can be overwhelming and become greed if not combined with generosity and gratitude. Knowing how to share makes all the difference.

AUTUMN

Autumn is the glory that comes after a full, juicy summer with its magnificent shades of reds, vermilions, and yellows. It shows off the richness of the leaves, yet when we go close, we find the fragility of their dryness. It is like discovering the early wrinkles on a face . . . the reflections of a life lived. We must embrace them!

ATTENTION

Once we pay attention to details and to others, our lives become richer. It's like adding colors to a drawing, turning it into a painting. Or, walking into a forest, some people will see trees. Others a universe.

ADVENTURE

Adventure is the discovery of the unknown. It is expanding our journey of learning and going beyond what is familiar.

ADVOCACY

Fight for the good, and the bad will disappear. Standing up against violence, abuse, and inequality, we must look for the light and build around it. Finding empathy inside us will help shift humanity. Advocacy is using our voice. It is our duty and a privilege do so. *See* HUMANITY.

AROMA

Aroma is a pleasure of the senses. The smell in the air, the perfume of the flower, the spice in the sauce . . . a touch of it makes all the difference.

ASSUMER

Assumer is the French word for *owning it.*

ATTITUDE
Attitude is everything—it is waving the flag of *owning it*.

AFFIRMATION
Affirmation is the *GO* button for *DO IT*. Focus on the intention, mean it, and *go*.

ANGER
Anger is the toxic demonstration of disagreement and suffering. It should be acknowledged and then released as a motivation to improve the situation.

ADDICTION
When pleasure becomes prison, it is addiction.

APPRECIATE
To appreciate is to savor the moment.

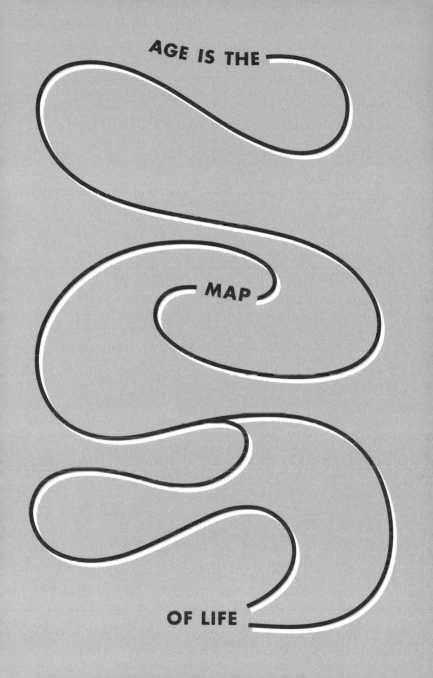

AGE IS THE MAP OF LIFE

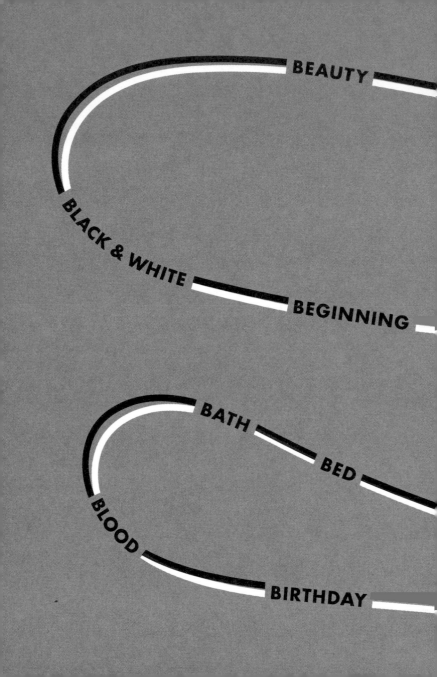

BEAUTY

BLACK & WHITE

BEGINNING

BATH

BED

BLOOD

BIRTHDAY

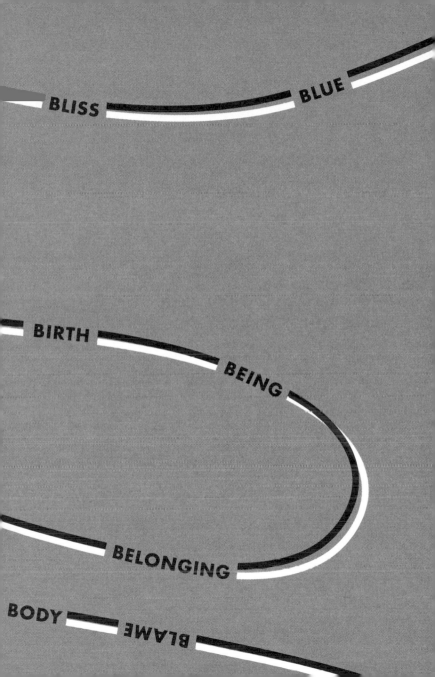

BLUE

Blue is nirvana, the color of meditation. It is also the color of the throat chakra—the color of our voice and self-expression.

My happiest moment is swimming far at sea into the horizon, getting lost in the blues . . . a tiny dot between the water and the sky.

BLISS

Bliss is a complete state of happiness. *See* HAPPINESS.

BEAUTY

Nothing has been more sought after or inspired people more than beauty. And no one has described beauty better than English poet John Keats, who wrote: "A thing of beauty is a joy forever" and "Beauty is truth, truth beauty." Beauty is what beauty does, and beauty is perfect in its imperfections.

BLACK & WHITE

I consider black and white together an essential color, as it makes every other color reveal its full potential.

BEGINNING

My adult life began with a bang. At twenty-two I got pregnant, married, moved to America, and started my company. It was a drastic beginning of life. The truth is, we celebrate a beginning every day as we put our feet on the ground.

BIRTH

Birth is the miracle of life . . . it is officially becoming a separate being, leaving the mother, having an independent identity. It is also a beginning, a reset.

Each time we reset—our journey, our priorities, our goals—it is a birth.

BEING

Being is existing, acknowledging ourselves as part of the universe. By accepting who we are, we own it!

BELONGING

Belonging can be a life's search. When we own who we are and belong to ourselves, we get stronger and the needy urge to belong elsewhere disappears. We can then also belong to others without getting lost. *See* COMMUNITY, FAMILY.

BED

My mother used to bless her bed every night: thankful for the sheets, the blanket, the pillow, and the warmth she had craved during her thirteen months of captivity during World War II, where all she had to sleep on was a wooden plank shared with rats. She gave me a sense of respect for the bed.

The bed is our most important ritual. It is where we are conceived, born, loved, lie sick and die. The bed is where we spend half our time . . . where we rest, dream, and refresh. *See* RITUALS.

BATH

The bath is a ritual in almost all religions, as water is a symbol of purification and hygiene. It is the ceremony of cleansing and renewal. Paying attention to that daily task adds a ceremonial awareness and appreciation. *See* RITUALS.

BLOOD

Blood is the intimidating red liquid that circulates inside our veins and arteries. It carries oxygen and nutrients to protect us against infection. Blood is a symbol for life; it is our fuel.

BIRTHDAY

A birthday is a time to celebrate and a perfect moment to assess, plan, and visualize who we want to be for the new year.

BODY

Our body is our physical self. We count on it and take it for granted, but it requires and deserves our love and care. We must learn how It works, appreciate its functions, respect it, and cherish it. Our body is also a language; the more at ease we are in it, the more attractive we look to others.

BLAME

Blame is a word to ban from our vocabulary. When we blame, we give up our power. Blaming is the opposite of owning it.

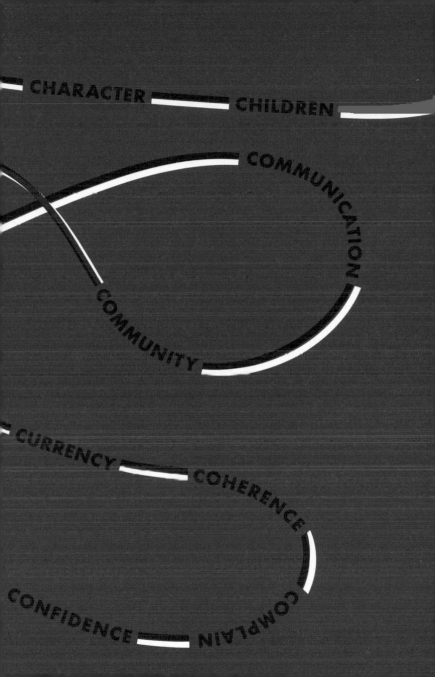

CHARACTER

Character is the one and only thing we have total control of.
We can lose our health, our wealth, our beauty, our family,
our freedom, but we never lose our character . . . even under
torture. Our character is our strength, our spinal cord,
the house inside ourselves—it's all we can truly count on!

CLARITY

Imagine a day with no visibility . . . then suddenly the fog
lifts and it's totally clear.

Clarity is seeing everything with focus and precision—
without it confusion reigns. It is a pursuit, a practice, and
a most wonderful achievement when we find it.

CONNECT

To connect is to use our magic wand to create the human
chain of love. It is paying attention to others, understanding
their needs, and knowing that a few words or a simple
introduction can change their lives.

Every morning I make sure I allocate quality time to
writing at least two emails that don't benefit me and spark
a connection for someone else. It's a simple, easy habit
and a use of our magic wand. *See* MAGIC, QUALITY TIME.

COMPASSION

I only learned about the meaning of the word *compassion*
after I was diagnosed with cancer at age forty-seven.
Until then, life had been a marathon.

I remember the waiting rooms, the fearful eyes. I
understood the suffering of others while refusing mine,
reaching for my own strength . . . *owning it.*

My treatment was eight weeks of daily radiation.
Although the treatment itself only took a few minutes,
there was always a long wait. The wait became an
opportunity for a routine, to find a book to read only
there, something that held me together. I picked a
story of a grandmother, mother, and daughter—three
generations of strong Chinese women who suffered
and survived extraordinarily difficult conditions, from
bonded feet to cultural revolution. I finished reading the
book exactly as I completed my treatment. By that time,
I understood compassion.

Compassion is an emotion, but also a muscle that
gets trained and developed. It is a practice that adds
a fuller dimension to identify with others and their
sufferings as well as our own. *See* EMPATHY, ROUTINE.

CEREMONY

The ceremony of life is the sacred way to give intention
and meaning to the most mundane and simple daily
tasks and turn them into full manifestations. *See* BATH,
BED, RITUALS, TABLE.

COMMUNITY

Community is a group of people linked by common values and needs to build a support system. We find our community by being authentic, intimate, and sharing vulnerability. When we build a community, we create power. *See* FAMILY.

COMMUNICATION

Communication must be treated seriously and with thoughtfulness, as it is the key to truth. It will help avoid misunderstandings and unhappiness. *See* TRUTH.

CREATIVITY

Creativity is the mysterious and magical manifestation of imagination and inventiveness. Even when it may appear frivolous, creativity leads to daring and to valuable experiment—never a waste. *See* RESTRICTIONS.

COHERENCE

I have great respect for coherence. Coherence is taking inventory of what we are and what we believe, making sure that all is aligned, fits together, and makes sense. It is reflected by how we run our lives, how we communicate with others, how we dress, what we read, and what we eat.

The more coherent, the happier we are—leaving room, of course, for a twist of contradiction and eccentricity that reveals our true personality.

COURAGE

Courage is using our character for strength It is the willingness to face danger, challenges, and emotions. We practice courage by managing fear and obstacles . . . Password: OWN IT See OBSTACLE.

COMMITMENT

A commitment is a pledge, a decision to do something and stick to it, even if we don't like it in the moment. It is the action of owning it.

CURRENCY

Currency is a way to measure and exchange our values. We should reflect on our human currency and use it more. *See* EMPATHY.

COMPLAIN

Complaining is a useless form of expression. It should be used as little as possible, as it is draining and attracts negativity.

COMPASS

A compass is a practical utensil that tells us exactly where we are. Our internal compass forces us to be honest with ourselves, a reminder of how not to get lost.

CONFIDENCE

Confidence is contagious both inside and out—it makes us beautiful. It is the form of expression that shows we fully accept who we are . . . it is owning it!

CLOUD

How can something that is nothing but condensed moisture be so beautiful? I love clouds—love to watch them and read their shapes to predict things about my day.

COOL

It's not cool to want to be cool. Being cool is owning who we are.

CHILDREN

I have seven children, counting my five grandchildren.

As all mothers do, I want more for them than I want for myself. I love them unconditionally and respect them, but also admire them, watching them go into life owning who they are.

As a young mother, I was worried to be too strong and have an overpowering voice, so I made sure to give them plenty of space to express theirs. I certainly succeeded in that, as I am now often lovingly belittled by them . . . however, my dream of them becoming who they want to be is fulfilled!

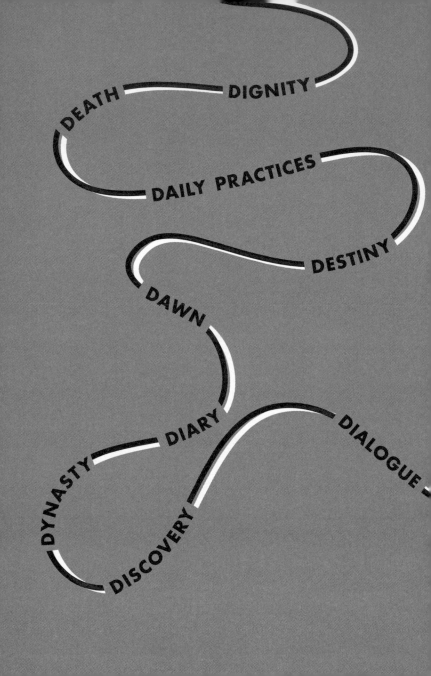

DEATH — DIGNITY

DAILY PRACTICES

DESTINY

DAWN

DIARY — DIALOGUE

DYNASTY

DISCOVERY

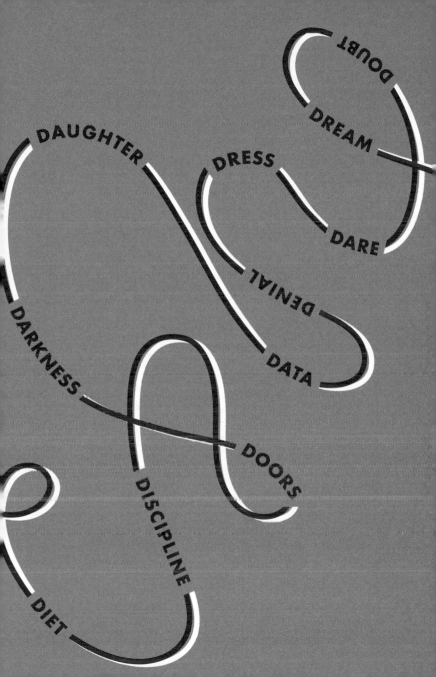

DOUBT

DREAM

DARE

DENIAL

DATA

DRESS

DAUGHTER

DARKNESS

DOORS

DISCIPLINE

DIET

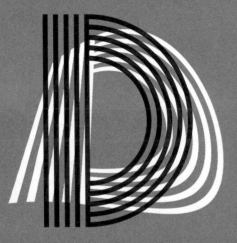

DIGNITY

Dignity is the gracious way we wear our character and values . . . true style! *See* CHARACTER.

DEATH

The moment of our death is a unique experience that should be lived and embraced, not feared or ignored. Knowing that death is inevitable forces us to think about it, live with it, and own it. I used to think that to die sleeping was the best death, but I am not so sure anymore.

My friend Lilou was Coco Chanel's last assistant. One night, Mademoiselle Chanel called her and asked her to come. "I am feeling strange," she said. "I think this is how death feels." When Lilou arrived a half hour later, she found her boss dying sitting in her favorite chair.

I love the image of the strong Coco Chanel, welcoming her last passage, determined to go as elegantly as she had always lived.

DAILY PRACTICES

As we open our eyes in the morning, we must practice being grateful.

Then we put our feet on the ground, optimistic, smiling at ourselves in the mirror, and welcome the day with all its challenges and opportunities. *See* RITUALS.

DESTINY

Beware of our thoughts as they become words,
Beware of our words as they become actions,
Beware of our actions as they become habits,
Beware of our habits as they become character,
Beware of our character as it becomes destiny.
—Author unknown

Destiny is not fully in our hands, but along the journey
of our lives we get signals, opportunities, and events that
allow us to make decisions to help design the path of
our lives. We must ride it with confidence and make
the best of it. *See* KISMET.

DAWN

Dawn is the magical moment when light pushes the
darkness away.

DIARY

I have kept a diary all my life. It has been my best friend,
my refuge, my confidant. It is where I share my anxieties,
my doubts, my dreams. It is where I express my gratitude
and my prayers. I seldom reread my diaries, but when I do,
I seem to always be at a turning point, as if all I ever did in
my life was turn!

DYNASTY

A few years ago, I visited a refugee camp in Thessaloniki, Greece. First, I went to the women's compound and chatted with them. The conversation was the same as I'd always had with women. We spoke about war, family, strength, and survival.

Later, I was driven to the "Unaccompanied Children Center." I was stunned. Those were not children. They were young men, teenagers, who had survived crossing the mountains of Syria, Iraq, and Iran.

We all sat under a big tree. I did not know what to say. I felt helpless, so, stupidly, I told them they were handsome.

"It may seem like that from the outside," one of the boys answered, "but inside we are sad."

"Sad?" I said. "You are heroes! Think of how much you have already overcome. I am sure you will have a successful life."

As we were leaving an hour later and about to get back on the bus, one of the young men followed me and said, "I will remember this tree."

So will I. That is when I understood that when we feel helpless in front of collective injustice and abuse, even if all we can do is help one life and one life only, it is well worth it. That one surviving refugee will start his own dynasty—all the hope for the world is carried in that future.

DISCOVERY

Discovery is the best and most magical way to learn.

DIALOGUE

A true dialogue is knowing how to give equal time and importance to who is speaking and to who is listening. *See* COMMUNICATION.

DIET

A healthy diet will make us look better, live longer, and feel stronger. Paying attention to what we put inside ourselves is a sign of self-respect and owning it.

DISCIPLINE

Discipline becomes character.

It is the mental and physical practice of respecting what we must do even when we don't want to. *See* CHARACTER.

DOORS

When we begin our adult lives, we are not sure what direction to take. Of all the doors ahead of us, which one to open? My door certainly was not a glamorous one. It was a gritty print factory near Como, Italy. There I learned all the tools of the trade that were to become my profession: designing. It was my lucky door.

DARKNESS

When I was a little girl, to teach me to conquer my fear of the dark, my mother locked me in a closet. It may appear cruel, but it worked. After a few minutes, I realized the dark never stays that dark. There is always a tiny bit of light. Chasing the fear, and always looking for light, is what it taught me—a lesson I never forgot.

DAUGHTER

To be a daughter and to have a daughter are very much the same thing. It's about needing love, giving it, sometimes resisting it, all unconditionally.

DATA

Data is the currency of the future. It creates the patterns that determine all decisions, but whatever happened to exceptions?

DRESS

I created a little dress, a wrap dress to be precise. Because it was a pretty, practical, sexy little dress, it became very popular and gave confidence to millions of women. I know I made the dress, but truly the dress made me! It gave me freedom, independence, identity, and confidence. *See* FASHION.

DENIAL

Denial is the opposite of owning it . . . it is the essence of being delusional, and a recipe for insecurity and failure.

DARE

Dare is one of my favorite words—it can be danger and risk, but it is also a sign of freedom and courage. It is a must-have in every toolbox, to be used in moderation.

DOUBT

When I doubt myself, I think of Honoré de Balzac, who said, "When you doubt your power, you give power to your doubt." *See* POWER.

DREAM

The dreams we have in our sleep are in the hands of our subconscious.

The dreams we have when awake are visions that we can make happen.

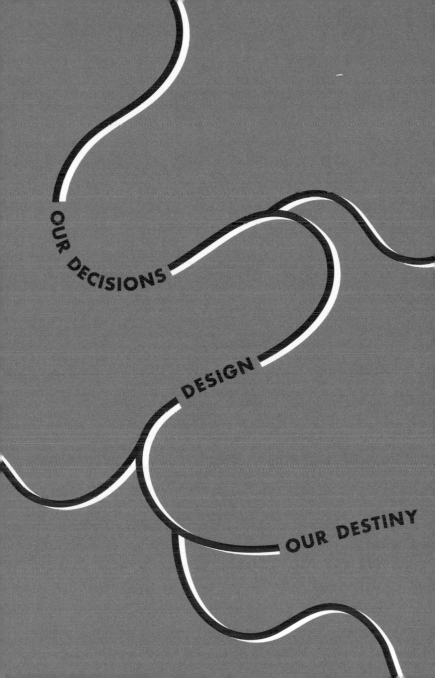

OUR DECISIONS

DESIGN

OUR DESTINY

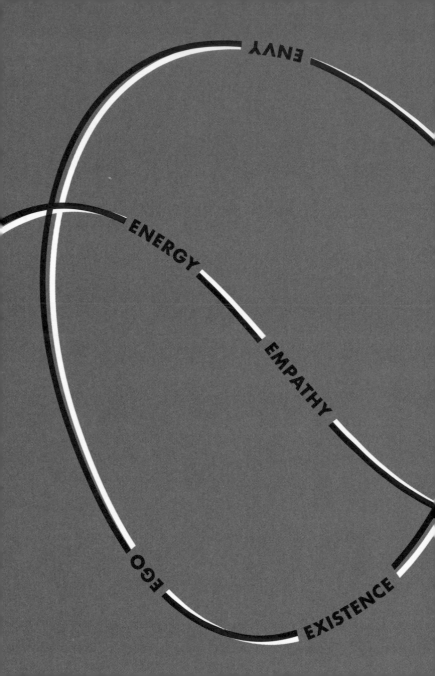

ENVY

ENERGY

EMPATHY

EGO

EXISTENCE

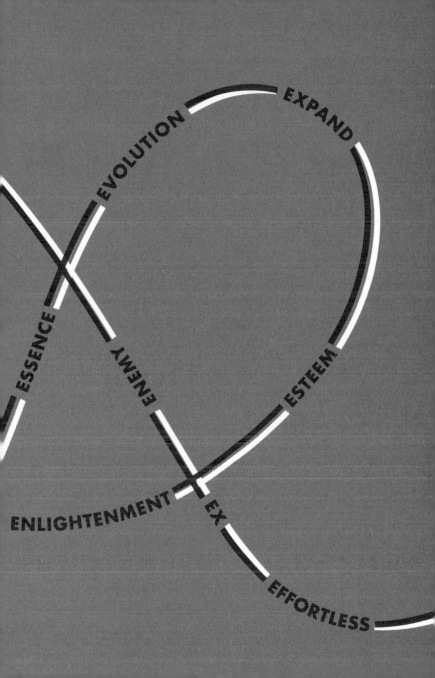

ENERGY

Strength, force, power . . . energy is a matter of both concentration and letting go. Energy is love, prayer, concentration.

When I wake up deflated and in doubt, I put my feet on the ground, welcome the day by feeling gratitude, and slowly feel the energy flowing in.

EMPATHY

Empathy is the ability to feel, share, and understand other people's sufferings and emotions. It is a practice, a habit, and a way of being. Empathy is the highest of human values because it nurtures compassion and kindness. If we all practiced empathy a little bit every day, we would shift the planet into human kindness. *See* COMPASSION, DISCIPLINE.

ENLIGHTENMENT

Enlightenment is the action of bringing light, individualism, freedom, and openness. It is the path to truth.

ESTEEM

Esteem is the respect and favorable appreciation that we have for someone. Self-esteem is when we apply it to ourselves. Having low self-esteem is the opposite of being InCharge and of owning it—none of us deserve it.

EXPAND

Expand is to stretch beyond.

The best way to expand our horizon is by discovering places or spending quality time with someone we normally would not connect with ... magic happens ... on both sides.

EVOLUTION

Nothing in nature is still. There is always consistent change, development, and growth. Being part of nature, we too evolve. It is important not to resist the flow. *See* NATURE.

ESSENCE

Essence is the extract of who we are, the undeniable core of someone or something.

EXISTENCE

Existence is the reality of being and the legitimacy of what we do.

EGO

Ego is a positive outlook on oneself that can easily become an unbearable flaw when abused. *See* NARCISSISM.

ENVY

Envy is a most toxic feeling that needs to be abolished. It only attracts negativity and is almost never justified . . . it's one of the seven deadly sins for good reason.

I have never dared to envy anyone because, being superstitious, I have always been afraid there would be something hidden that I would not want. *See* JEALOUSY.

ENEMY

By declaring someone an enemy, we give them power. The best way to neutralize them is to ignore them . . . or seduce them. *See* VICTORY.

EX

I believe in cherishing our exes. I find the souvenirs and intimacy we shared reassuring.

EFFORTLESS

Effortless is what owning it looks like, even though it is hard work.

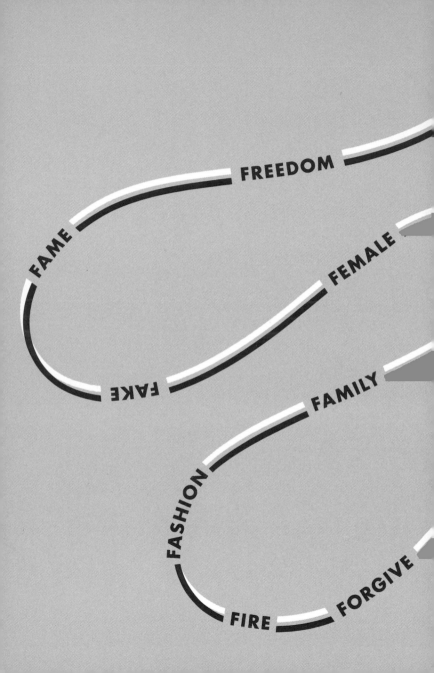

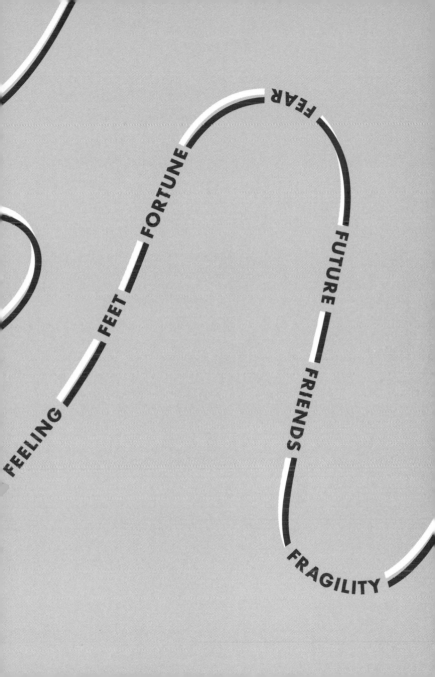

FREEDOM

Freedom is being able to be, to feel and to speak without restriction . . . it is also being able to pay the bills. As exhilarating as freedom is, it is imperative to remember that our freedom stops when it infringes on someone else's. I feel the freest when no one knows where I am. I call these special moments "stolen moments."

FAME

The best thing about fame is that it gives us a voice to amplify. It is being recognized, respected, and acclaimed.

My favorite fame story happened in Kathmandu, Nepal. I was being hosted by my Nepalese fellow designer Prabal Gurung. We were in the middle of a holy week, and the monks had been chanting for days. We went to the sacred Seto Gumba, also known as the White Monastery, and as very privileged guests, we sat by the shrine close to the spiritual leader, or *Rinpoche*, which translates as "precious one." I felt humbled to be there and totally excited when I was invited to meet this holy man. After the first introduction, he turned to me and asked, "Do you know Cher?" I was taken by surprise but proud to tell him that, "Yes, I do know Cher."

I will never forget this story, as it will be forever the most unexpected anecdote about the power, and the silliness, of fame.

FAKE

Being fake is like having an impostor living inside ourselves, bringing only insecurity, unhappiness, and endless misunderstandings. *See* IMPOSTOR.

FEMALE

I have always been proud to be female. We are the ones who produce the eggs, give life, and nurture.

Women are very strong, although we often forget it or pretend we are not.

FAMILY

We cannot choose our parents. We probably like where we land, but if we don't, we simply have to make the best of it. Later, however, we make our chosen family of friends, partners, spouses, and children. The family we are born into and the family we make are both reflections of who we are; it is our tribe, our shelter, and our strength. *See* FRIENDS.

FIRE

Fire is an essential element and powerful force, a symbol of undeniable strength, power, and destruction.

Distance is to love what wind is to fire: it extinguishes the small flames and amplifies the big ones.

FASHION

Fashion is the image of the time, the zeitgeist. It displays the tastes of the moment, the lifestyle, the clothes, the shoes, the hair, the makeup, the cars, the architecture, the food, the manners, the habits.

My role in fashion has always been about the woman and the woman first. How to make her feel good and in charge, helping her to be the woman she wants to be. It's about how she feels, using the tricks of dressmaking, the colors, the fluidity of the fabric, the prints. All of it creates the secret body language of confidence. *See* DRESS, IN CHARGE.

FORGIVE

When we forgive, we free ourselves. Resentment and anger are forms of attachment. To forgive is not to forget, but it is the ultimate sign of letting go.

FEELING

Feeling is the mother of all our emotions, a manifestation of how we react. It affects our behavior and health.

FEET

I love my legs, but I count on my feet. Feet are our anchor, our connection to the earth.

FORTUNE

Fortune is a good omen, luck, and positive energy.

FEAR

Fear is not an option. When we push fear aside, the situation remains the same, but it becomes more manageable.

FUTURE

The future that follows the present is a path not yet taken. We cannot own the future, but we can visualize it and try to make it happen. *See* PRESENT, TIME.

FRIENDS

Friends are the most valuable and enriching relationships we have. Friends are the family we choose to share with and care for—logical family versus biological family. Of course, our most reliable friend is ourself! *See* FAMILY.

FRAGILITY

Accepting our fragility makes us strong.

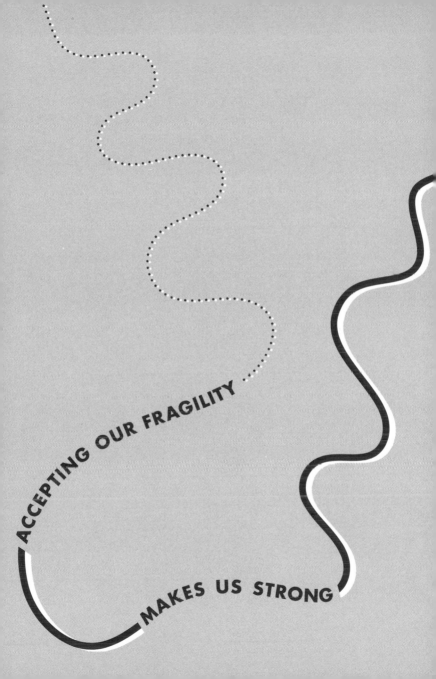

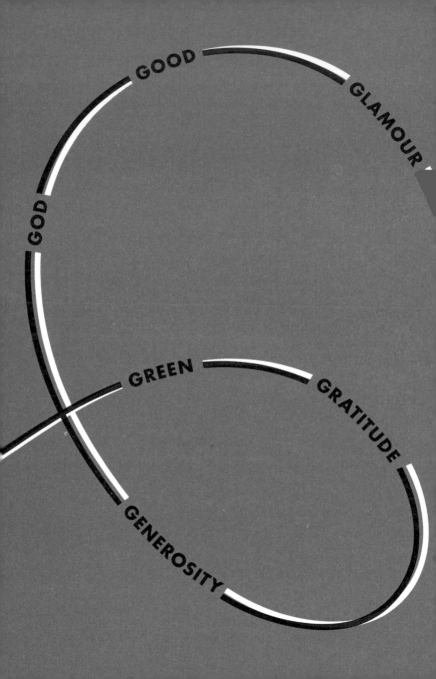

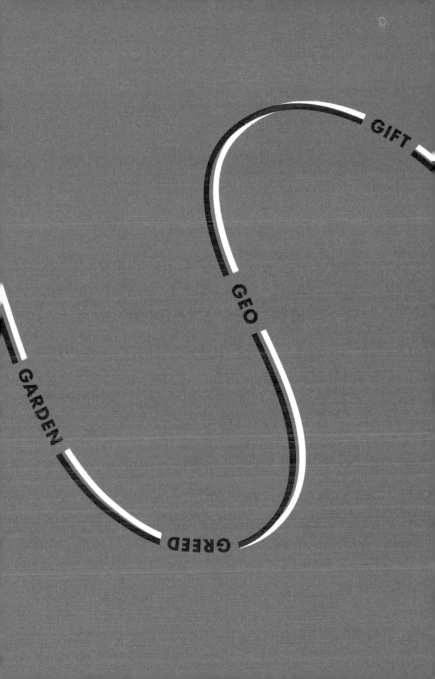

GREEN

Green is the color of nature, the color of life, a symbol of growth.

GRATITUDE

Saying thank you as we open our eyes gives us a better day. Nourishing gratitude inside ourselves, even in the most challenging moments, is a source of strength.

GENEROSITY

Generosity is the best investment. Sharing is a privilege that makes us richer.

GOD

God is everything and everywhere.

GOOD

Good is God with two Os. We can never be too good, and good is never bad.

GARDEN

A garden is a curated piece of land to grow flowers, herbs, or vegetables. To cultivate our inner garden is knowing how to improve ourselves and to design our lives.

GLAMOUR

Glamour is shine, polish, mystery . . . it adds a fascinating appeal and magical touch to individuals or situations.

It is a word I use all the time. All I ever wanted was to be glamorous. It started, at the age of thirteen, by never being seen outside without wearing sunglasses. Later it was wearing the highest heels with fishnet stockings at all times, including in airports. Or, the slickest bias-cut, movie-star slips, and the easiest silk jersey dresses that make no noise when you undress—although the bangle bracelet does!

Is it an accident that the word *glamour* has *amour* in it?

GREED

Greed is the exaggerated desire for food, wealth, and power. A sin, for sure.

GEO (-GRAPHY, -LOGY, -METRY)

I love all sciences related to the earth . . . the earth we take for granted and must protect! I always wanted to go into space to be able to see the planet Earth as a little ball. Feeling tiny puts everything in perspective.

GIFT

It is no coincidence that the gift of life comes from an act of love. Nor that the "gift" is also called the "present."

TO CULTIVATE OUR INNER GARDEN

IS TO DESIGN OUR LIVES

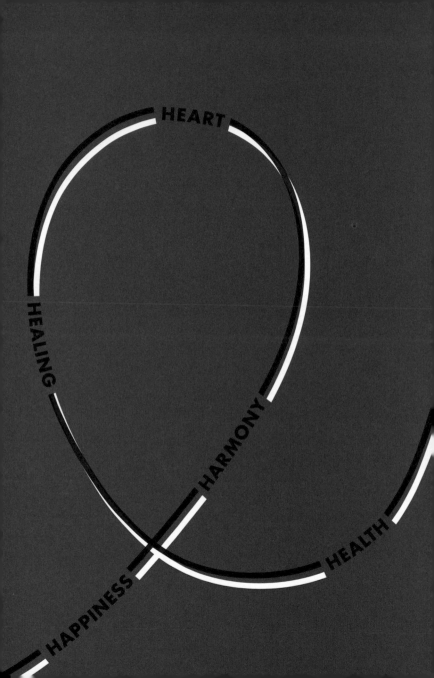

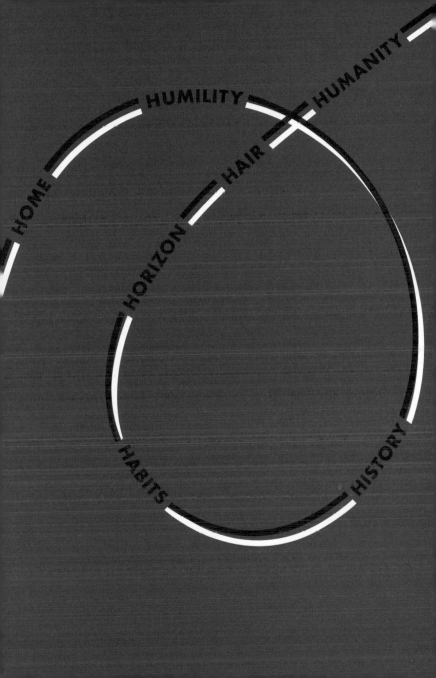

HAPPINESS

Happiness is to life what weather is to nature: never still. It constantly evolves and can change at any moment. So the more we are grateful, the more we go with the flow and enjoy the present, the happier we are.

HARMONY

Harmony is a combination of separate parts that together create balance, symmetry, and beauty. An indispensable pursuit, it can be applied to anything.

HEART

The heart is a muscle, and its beat is the first and most consistent sign of life. Life is love and love is life. Don't we make life by making love?

HEALING

Healing is the process of restoring health ... accepting the wound, visualizing the illness, and owning it help the healing.

HEALTH

Health is freedom. It cannot be taken for granted and needs attention, care, and love.

HOME

Home is the <u>shelter</u> we create for ourselves and our loved ones, and it reflects who we are. Our true home is the relationship we have with ourselves. Once we have that, it creates a <u>refuge</u> inside us that is the <u>core</u> of our strength.

HUMILITY

Humility is <u>NOT</u> about being small. By dismissing arrogance and embracing <u>compassion</u>, humility becomes strength and power.

HISTORY

History is the most interesting subject to learn. The minute something is no longer in the present, it becomes history. By <u>living fully</u> every moment of our lives, by focusing and applying our intention, we make our own history and become both the student and <u>legend of our lives.</u> *See* PAST.

HABITS

Habits can be good or bad. They reveal our <u>character</u> and determine our <u>destiny.</u> *See* RITUALS, DESTINY.

HORIZON

The horizon is the imaginary line that links the earth or the sea with the sky. It is a place for <u>wishes</u> and <u>dreams</u> to land.

HAIR

Hair is our most valued head decoration, for which we spend extraordinary amounts of time and money.

As a young girl in Belgium, I hated my dark, curly hair. All the other girls had long, blond, straight hair, and mine was unmanageable, especially with the constant Brussels rain. I spent long hours ironing it and avoiding humidity.

At twenty-eight, at the peak of success, I had my picture taken by my friend Ara Gallant, a photographer and previously a hairdresser, for the cover of *Interview*. My hair was long and straight, and I felt beautiful. After we finished, he took a water sprayer and started wetting my hair. "What are you doing?" I screamed. I was horrified. Ara was smiling, reassuring me that we already had the cover but insisting he wanted to try something else. I surrendered and posed for another twenty minutes while my wet hair was drying, naturally revealing its curls.

A few days later he proudly proposed to the magazine two cover trials: one with straight hair and another one much wilder with my wet, curly hair. The wild one won with enthusiasm, and since that day I have worn my hair the way nature intended.

I realized curly hair was who I was. Whether I liked it or not, I had to *own it.* Like a rite of passage, this acceptance of myself changed my life! *See* CONFIDENCE, IMAGE.

HUMANITY

Humanity describes the human race but also <u>kindness</u> and the ability to <u>love</u> and to have <u>compassion.</u>

It is important to remember that being human is what links us all together, and empathy will <u>save us</u>. Making room for other people's vulnerability as well as our own will make a better society, just as humanity's respect for nature will make a safer planet.

To think about humanity on a <u>daily basis</u> and contribute to its health should become a dedicated practice, a natural ritual. *See* COMPASSION.

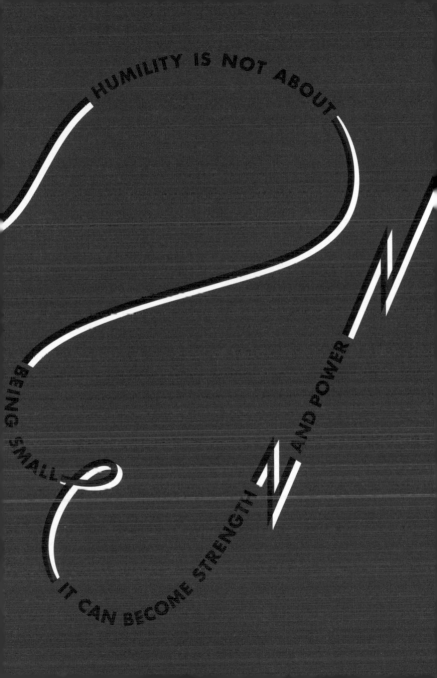

HUMILITY IS NOT ABOUT BEING SMALL. IT CAN BECOME STRENGTH AND POWER

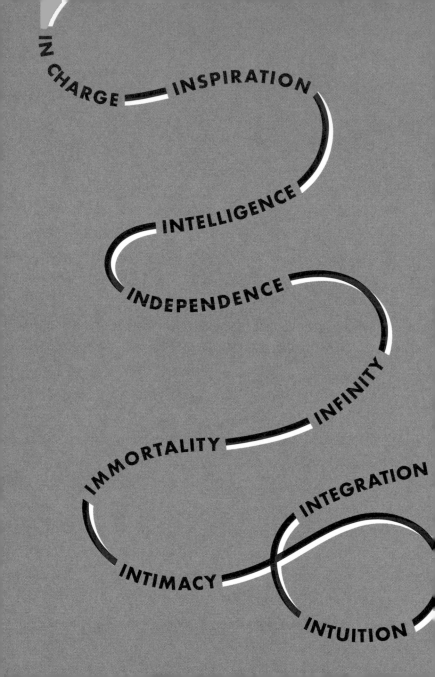

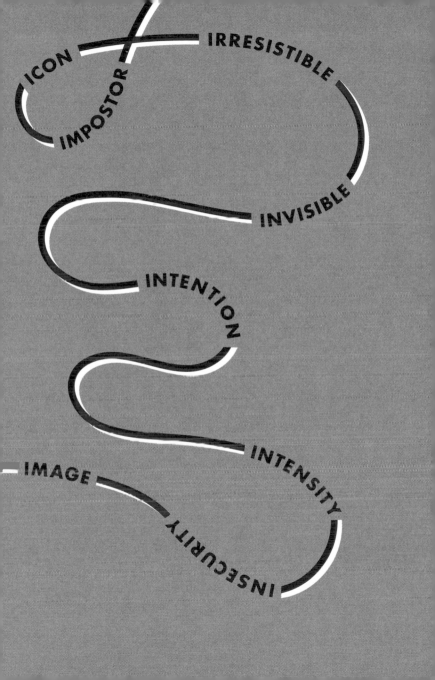

IN CHARGE

To be InCharge is first and foremost a commitment to ourselves. It is accepting who we are and owning it. We own our imperfections, they become our assets. We own our vulnerability, it becomes our strength. To be InCharge is about the relationship with ourselves. It is about our character; it is the shelter, the home inside ourselves. It is the core of our strength. Once InCharge, we are better able to connect, expand, inspire, and advocate.

INSPIRATION

Inspiration is the invisible energy and enthusiasm that awakens emotions, creativity, and ideas. We must trust it.

INTELLIGENCE

Knowledge, judgment, skill, and purpose combined with curiosity and open-mindedness make the foundation of intelligence. A sign of intelligence is to know how little we know. *See* KNOWLEDGE.

INDEPENDENCE

Independence is my reason for being. Growing up, I did not know what I wanted to do, but I knew the kind of woman I wanted to be: an independent woman who could design her own life. As a mother, what I wanted most was for my children to be responsible and therefore independent.

INFINITY

I find comfort in the magnitude of infinity—a space that goes forever and is as limitless as the universe. *See* UNIVERSE.

IMMORTALITY

We all aspire to it, but is there such thing as immortality? What is our legacy? Our children and those who come after them? Our body of work? We spend our lives creating an image and a persona . . . what lasts after we go?

The best way to make sure our lives have mattered is by doing as much good as possible and making a difference for others.

INTIMACY

I despise small talk and love intimacy. We don't have to know someone well to be intimate; we only need to break the barriers, go deep, and pay attention to their feelings as our own. Intimacy can build empathy.

INTUITION

Intuition is a feeling that comes freely without reasoning. Trusting intuition adds music to life and can be substantive.

INTEGRATION

Integration is the perfect way of merging body, soul, and mind and yet keeping them independent.

IMAGE

Our image is the vision we want to project. How we dress, speak, walk, eat, and decorate our rooms reflects how we design our image.

INSECURITY

Insecurity is a waste of time but can be used as a source for growth.

INTENSITY

Intensity is a condition of extreme concentration and emotion.

INTENTION

Memorable advice from Yang Yang, the Taiji master:

> When we focus on power, we get hurt,
> When we focus on energy, we stagnate,
> But when we focus on intention, we get
> power and energy.

See ENERGY, POWER.

INVISIBLE

The extraordinary thing about seeing the invisible is that it is the first draft to creativity and manifestation. *See* CREATIVITY.

IRRESISTIBLE

To be irresistible is to be overwhelmingly tempting or seductive.

ICON

Andy Warhol, who was very religious, loved the rich iconography represented in the Christian Orthodox Church. This love inspired him to create the modern icons by painting the celebrated and famous people he admired. I was honored to have him paint my portrait twice, in 1974 and in 1982.

He used to say anyone can be famous for fifteen minutes and, with that, popularized the world of celebrities. He painted movie stars, musicians, athletes, first ladies, and royalty, as well as everyday iconic brands. What a prophet he was and how amused he would be to witness the age of social media and influencers, where everyone is making themselves an icon. *See* FAME.

IMPOSTOR

Impostors make the best characters in books and movies. They are made of lies and denials that only bring trouble—confirmation that owning it and practicing the truth are the only ways to go. *See* DENIAL.

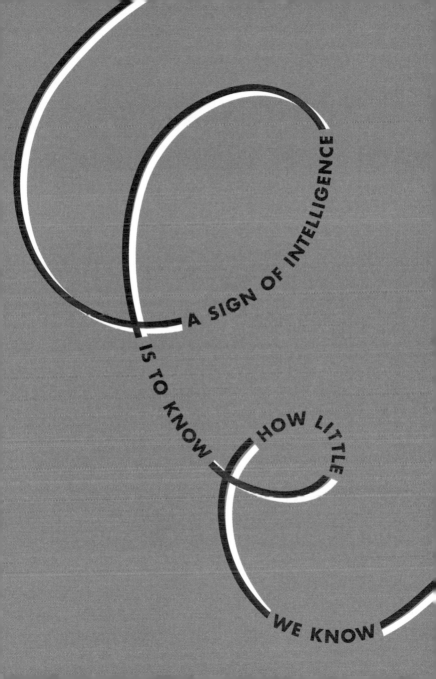

A SIGN OF INTELLIGENCE IS TO KNOW HOW LITTLE WE KNOW

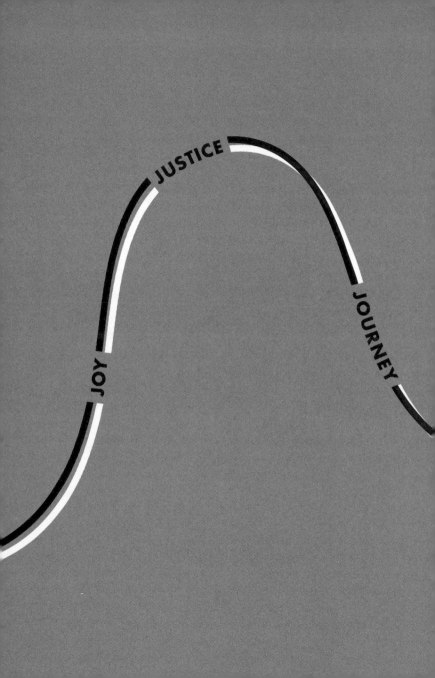

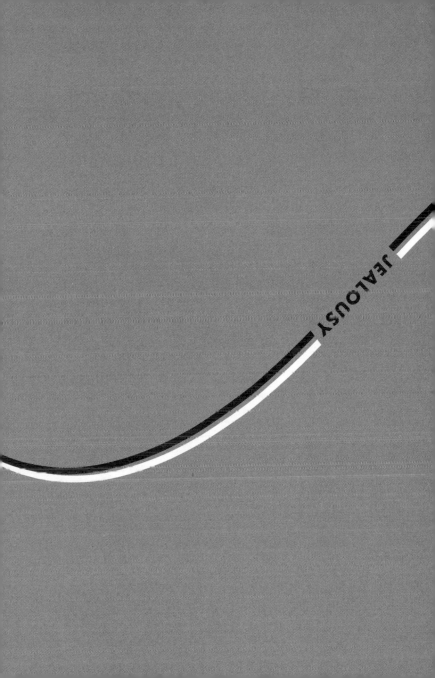

JEALOUSY

JOY

Joy is the explosion of happiness and pleasure.

JUSTICE

Justice is the practice of being fair and respecting the law. It is fighting against abuse, violence, and inequality. Justice is a condition for the well-being of society, humanity, and each of us individually. *See* ADVOCACY.

JOURNEY

The Talmud says: "Birth is a beginning and death a destination; but life is a journey."

Knowing that there is an end reminds us to enjoy the journey more and embrace every moment along the way.

JEALOUSY

Jealousy is a very toxic feeling that should be pushed away. Never comparing ourselves to others, and instead focusing on being the best we can be, will free us from jealousy.

My personal recommendation to avoid jealousy is never to ever look at anyone's phone or personal mail— nothing to gain there! *See* ENVY.

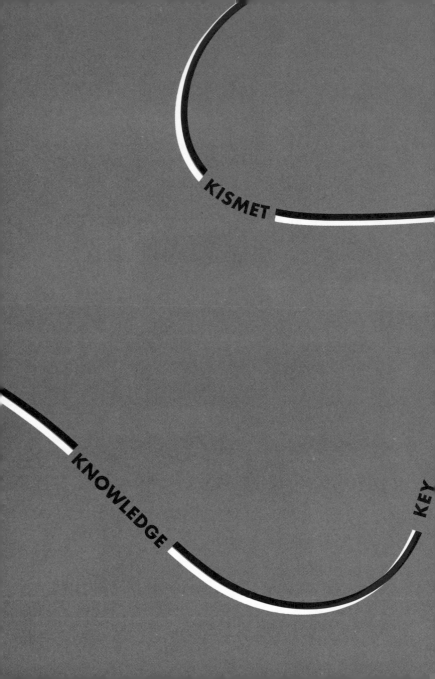

KISMET

KNOWLEDGE

KEY

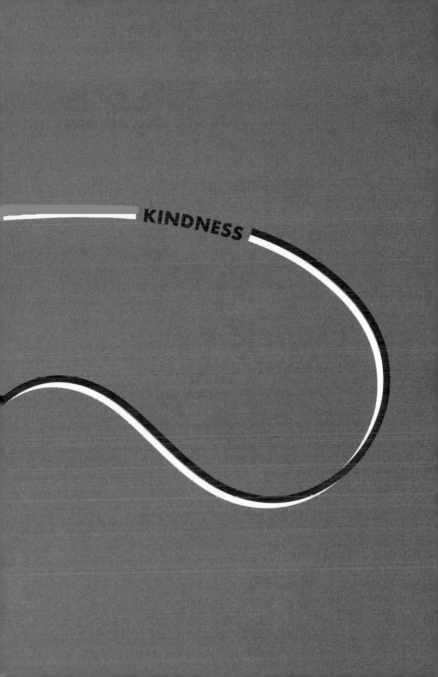

KINDNESS

KNOWLEDGE

Knowledge is the body of all the things we have learned and experienced.

Our knowledge is the library inside us. The more orderly, the easier to get to. To know is to *own it. See* INTELLIGENCE.

KEY

Even though a key is meant to lock, it is mostly the formula to open, access, and discover.

KINDNESS

Kindness can never be overrated . . . it's the way to protect others while protecting ourselves along the way. There should be a currency for kindness.

KISMET

Kismet is our destiny, our fate—not much we can do to change it. *See* DESTINY.

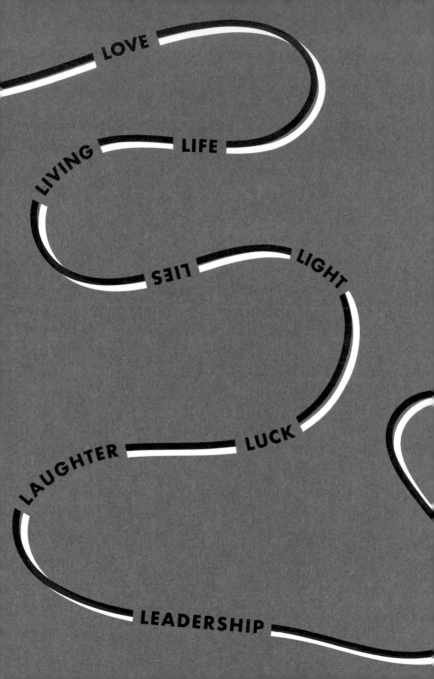

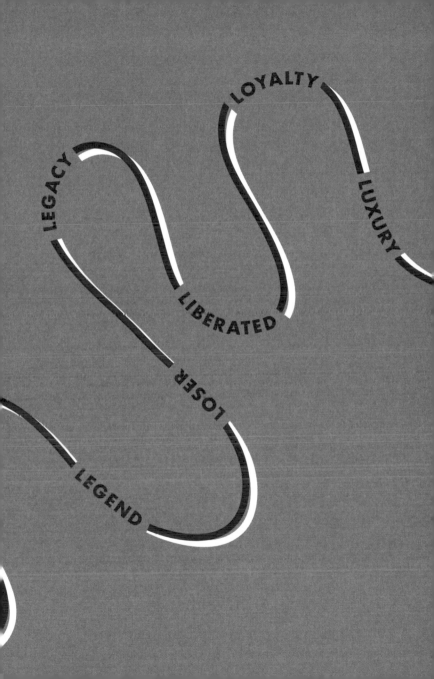

LOVE

Love is life. Life is love. There is no way to envision life without love. Nothing is more important. Love is caring, sharing, and giving unconditionally. It is being thankful and paying attention to others. Love is owning it.

LIFE

Life is existing, growing, creating, and owning it.

LIVING

I prefer the word *living* to the word *aging*. *See* AGE.

LIES

Lying is the enemy, the source of unhappiness and all things negative. I have never lied and hopefully never will. *See* TRUTH.

LIGHT

Light is magical. It changes everything, adds dimension, detail, perspective, and beauty. To look for light is an indisputable pursuit for wisdom and truth.

LUCK

Luck is an invisible protection and a friendly wink to our destiny. *See* FORTUNE.

LAUGHTER
Laughter is a healthy and pleasant demonstration of joy.
It is said that to laugh every day will lengthen your life.
See HAPPINESS.

LEADERSHIP
Leadership is knowing how to inspire others to fulfill
their tasks. It's about setting an example that others
can follow.

LEGEND
We can all be our own legend. It starts with a dream
that we turn into reality. *See* DREAM, IMMORTALITY.

LOSER
I sometimes feel like one, and then I remind myself,
only losers don't feel like losers.

LEGACY
Legacy is what we leave behind that others can use.
See IMMORTALITY.

LIBERATED

To be liberated is freeing ourselves from constraints and restrictions, bringing an enormous sense of lightness.

Women's liberation is the movement that I grew up with, and I will always carry its flame in my heart and in my actions. *See* FREEDOM.

LOYALTY

Loyalty to our own character is a priority and a source of strength. Loyalty to others is respecting them. *See* CHARACTER.

LUXURY

Luxury is elegance and refinement that goes beyond the essential. It is also serenity, silence, and space. *See* SERENITY.

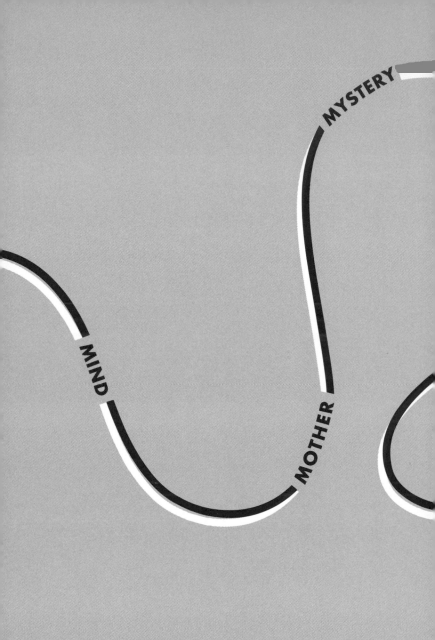

MYSTERY

MIND

MOTHER

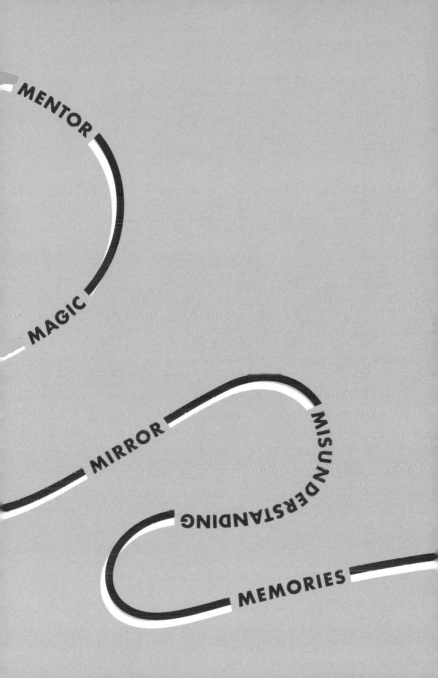

MENTOR

MAGIC

MIRROR

MISUNDERSTANDING

MEMORIES

MOTHER

Nature is the greatest mother, as it gives birth to everything.

Eighteen months before I was born, my mother was liberated from the Nazi concentration camps. She weighed forty-nine pounds and could barely move. Back in Belgium, her mother fed her bit by bit with food and love. Five months later, her fiancé came back from Switzerland, where he had spent the latter years of the war, and they were married. Her doctor warned them not to have a child, yet I came to life. My life was truly a miracle, as was my mother's survival.

My mother was strict and demanding, forbidding me ever to be afraid or to feel like a victim. It was not easy to be her daughter, but I was always thankful to her. By being tough and forcing me to be responsible, she gave me strength and freedom. To be a mother is to know how to protect, and the best way to protect is to give the child the keys of independence.

As for me, I became an adult and a very young mother at the same time, so it all blended together. As I became responsible because I had children, I made them responsible and free to be themselves. *See* INDEPENDENCE.

MIND

Our mind gives us the faculty of consciousness, of being able to think and make the right decisions. It holds our bank of memories and records our feelings. The more we are honest with ourselves, the clearer the mind grows and the more reliable it is.

MYSTERY

Mystery provokes the desire to discover, unveil the unknown. It is very seductive. *See* ALLURE.

MENTOR

I like to think that mentors give us keys. Each key can open something, but in ourselves we have the master key that can open everything. *See* KEY.

MAGIC

We all have a magic wand, and the more we use it, the more powerful it becomes. I do think our magic wand works best when we do good for others, but since doing good almost always comes back to us, it is fair to say that our magic wand can become a boomerang! *See* CONNECT.

MISUNDERSTANDING

Misunderstanding causes unhappiness and accidents. The best way to avoid it is to practice the truth. *See* TRUTH.

MEMORIES

Memories weave the most colorful carpet of images and emotions to lie on forever.

MIRROR

I know that liking mirrors can be seen as a sign of vanity, but for me a mirror has always offered a way to find myself. Looking at the mirror forces me to penetrate and own my truth.

I remember the large mirror in my mother's bedroom; I stared into it for hours. Not because I liked how I looked— I looked so different from my Belgian classmates, who were all blond with straight hair—but because the mirror showed me that my image could do anything I wanted it to do. If I lifted my arms, the girl in the mirror did the same. If I smiled, if I frowned, if I danced . . . she did too. The mirror showed me that I had control over me. Later, the mirror became the friend I check on, wink at, and wave to. *See* REFLECTION.

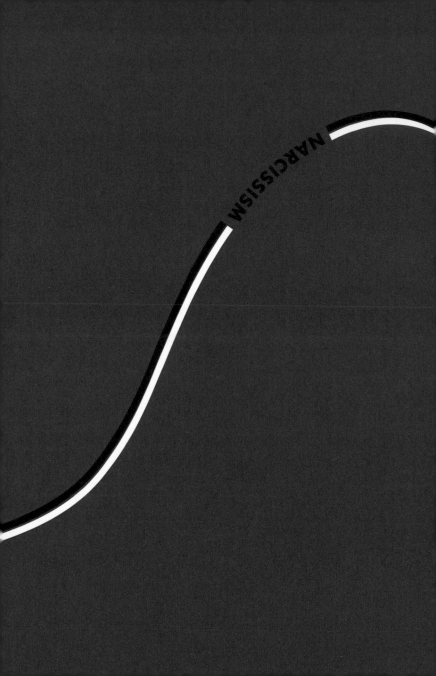

NARCISSISM

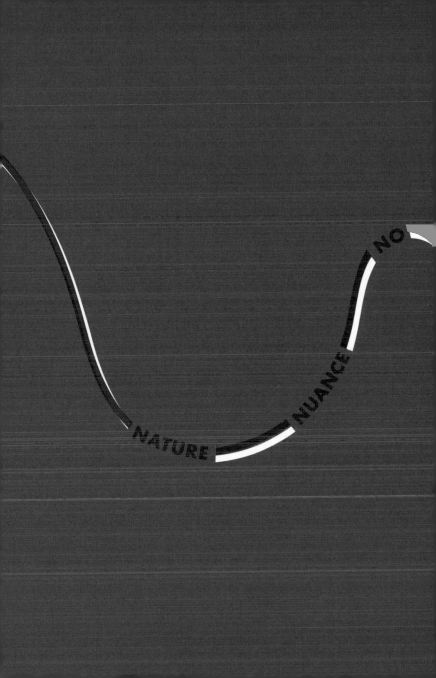

NARCISSISM

Narcissism is a cognitive prison of our own making. It is being delusional about who we are and actually loving it—NOT an attractive trait. *See* EGO.

NATURE

Nature is *EVERYTHING*. Everything we eat, build, and use comes from nature. We take it for granted, we abuse it, and yet we totally depend on it. Nature is the source of life, of energy, and of beauty. It is never static; it evolves and always continues to amaze us.

Leonardo da Vinci, the greatest mind of all time, used to say that the thing he was most proud of among all his accomplishments was that "he could read nature."

NUANCE

Nuances are subtle shades of anything and everything.

To notice and live them is a very refined and fun way to experience our life.

NO

Saying no is making a decision, it is being InCharge. *See* IN CHARGE.

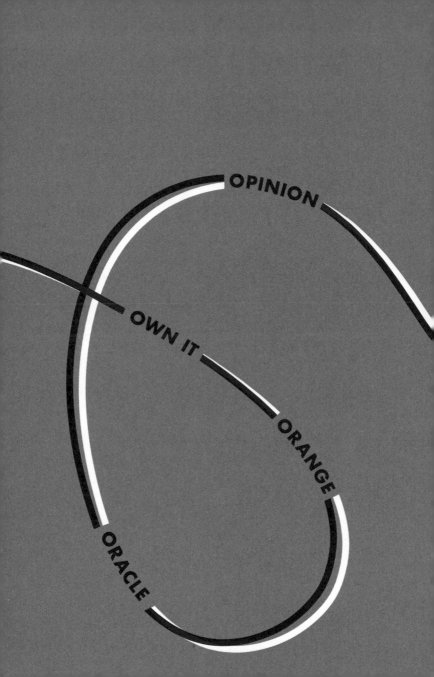

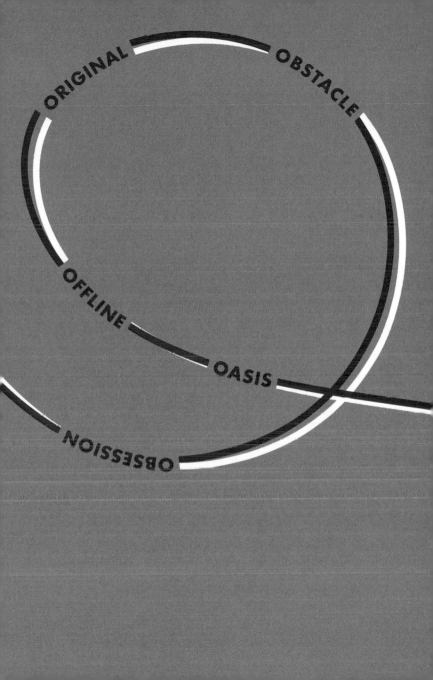

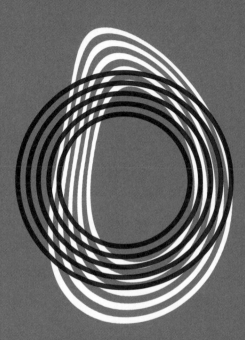

OWN IT

The more I think about it, the more I think owning it is the key for everything, the secret to life. It applies to everything and everyone. It is about assuming responsibility, accepting reality, and dealing with the truth.

ORANGE

Orange is created when yellow and red mix. It is the color of the sunset and of autumn—the transition between day and night and summer and fall. *See* AUTUMN.

ORACLE

My fantasy has always been to be an oracle. Fascinated by Greek antiquity, I dreamt of being a goddess with the powers of seduction, goodness, and knowledge. Now, as I am in the sunset of my very full life, I enjoy using my experience, my knowledge, and my voice to help others as I have helped myself.

OPINION

An opinion is a point of view, judgment, or report about something not always based on facts. Hear everybody's opinions and then listen to our own hearts would be my advice. *See* POINT OF VIEW.

OBSESSION

Obsession is an exaggerated passion than can create drive but also cause us to crash and to hurt.

OBSTACLE

Obstacles are part of our journey; each one is a teacher.

ORIGINAL

An original is the truest manifestation of anything or anyone. Originals are authentic and genuine—not copies. *See* AUTHENTICITY, FAKE.

OFFLINE

To be offline means not being connected; yet the most important connection is the one we have with ourselves. *See* CONNECT.

OASIS

An oasis is an area of water, fertility, and life in the middle of the desert, a place for unexpected hope, calm, and infinite possibilities.

To OWN IT is to create an oasis inside ourselves.

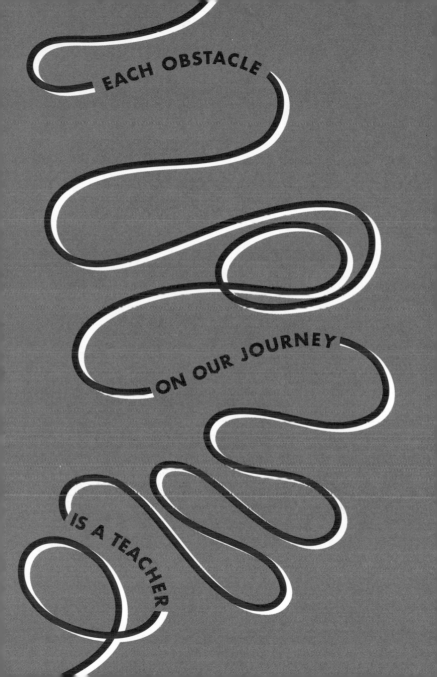

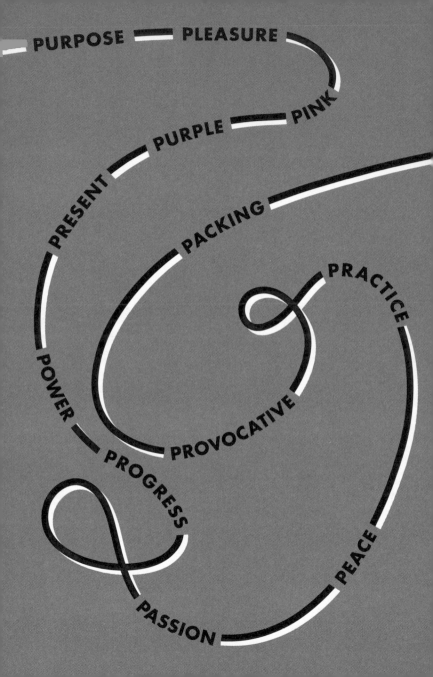

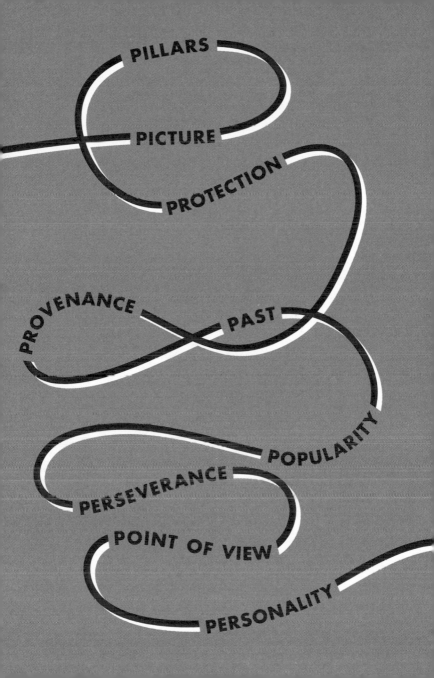

PILLARS

PICTURE

PROTECTION

PROVENANCE

PAST

POPULARITY

PERSEVERANCE

POINT OF VIEW

PERSONALITY

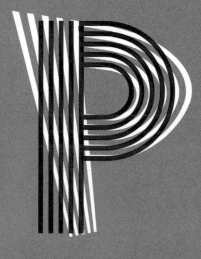

PURPOSE
Purpose has a wider scope than an intention; it is more than a mere goal and bigger than ourselves. Purpose radiates. My purpose is to empower every woman to feel InCharge. *See* INDEPENDENCE, IN CHARGE.

PLEASURE
Pleasure is letting go into realms of enjoyment and embracing feelings.

PINK
Pink is what white does to red. It is the most feminine and flirtatious of all colors. *See* RED.

PURPLE
Purple is what blue does to red. It is a color we either love or hate.

PRESENT
The gift of now is called the present.

To be present is to be aware and conscious of the moment. To live in the present is a recipe for happiness. *See* AWARENESS.

POWER

A symbol of strength, power can be an aphrodisiac. The more you taste it, the more you want it. And, you need to really want it to have it.

Power brings influence but needs to be handled with care, as it can be dangerous. *See* ADDICTION.

PROGRESS

Progress is evolution: the result of work toward intention.

PASSION

Passion is the powerful and uncontrollable essence of emotions.

PEACE

Peace is the full acceptance of calm. It is freedom from disruption and a state of contemplation. Peace is always good.

PRACTICE

Practice is the application of belief, repeated exercise, and discipline. All practice is progress. *See* DISCIPLINE.

PROVOCATIVE

Provocative is one of my favorite words; I love the sound of it—it tickles. It is a combination of question and affirmation.

Nothing is more provocative than speaking the truth and revealing our imperfections. The provocative part gets the attention, but the truth gets respect.

When I first started my company in my early twenties, I did a lot of personal appearances all around the country. Los Angeles, Philadelphia, Detroit, Miami, San Francisco . . . it was all so new and exotic to me. "A young European Park Avenue Princess coming to town to show her easy, affordable little dresses," is how I was introduced by the local press everywhere. I did not love that definition. That's when I decided to become a bit more provocative in my narrative, to show that I was not perfect. The words became mine and the story no longer a fairy tale.

PACKING

Since life is a journey, when we know how to pack, we know how to live . . . pack lightly, live lightly.

PICTURE

If you don't like a picture of yourself now, all you need to do is wait ten years—you will love it then!

PILLARS

I imagine the Temple of Life with seven pillars of wisdom supporting it:

Nature, the source of everything.
Character, the only thing we can control.
Body, Soul, and Mind, which represent us in all parts.
Heart, our engine.
Image, the reflection of who we are.
Rituals, the ceremony of how we do things.

PROTECTION

There is no better feeling of protection than knowing you can count on yourself.

PROVENANCE

Provenance is adding value to something by finding its origin and history. It is an interesting word that can add cachet and relevance to a person too.

PAST

The past is defined as no longer existing . . . yet we carry it into the present and the future. *See* HISTORY, PRESENT.

POPULARITY

Popularity is the state of being liked, admired, followed, or desired by many. It gives us the (power) to amplify our voice. It should, therefore, be used responsibly.

PERSEVERANCE

Perseverance is the combination of will and discipline, a key to success. *See* DISCIPLINE, KEY.

POINT OF VIEW

To be open-minded and make our own decisions, we need to pay attention to all points of view, especially the ones we don't agree with. *See* OPINION.

PERSONALITY

Personality is wearing who we are, it is owning it.

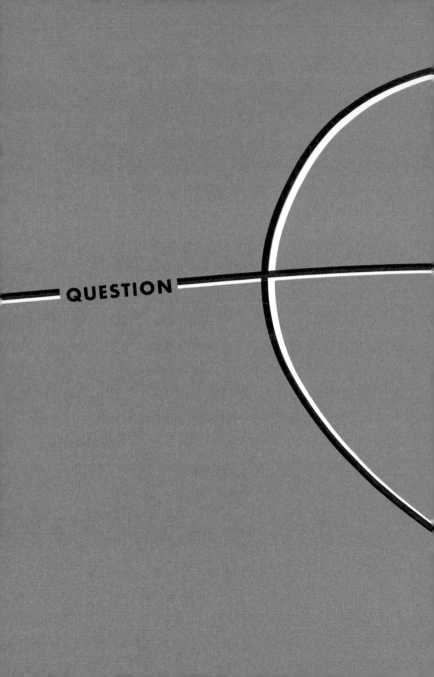
QUESTION

QUOTE

QUALITY TIME

QUIET

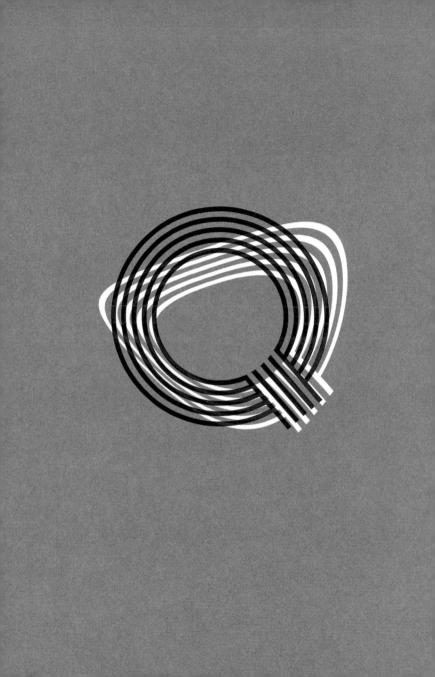

QUESTION

To raise a question is the first step to getting an answer. To question is curiosity, intelligence, and humility.

It's been said before, but it's absolutely true, the only wrong question is the one that isn't asked. *See* INTELLIGENCE, KNOWLEDGE.

QUALITY TIME

Quality time means limiting distraction and fully owning the moment.

It is a luxurious gift.

QUIET

To be quiet can be the loudest thing we do.

QUOTE

I have spent my life believing that every word matters.

A good quote has the ability to make us feel and be inspired . . . we can hold onto a quote forever. *See* WORDS.

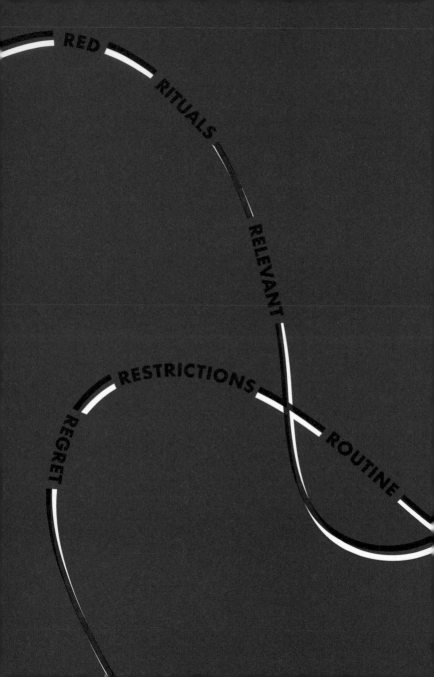

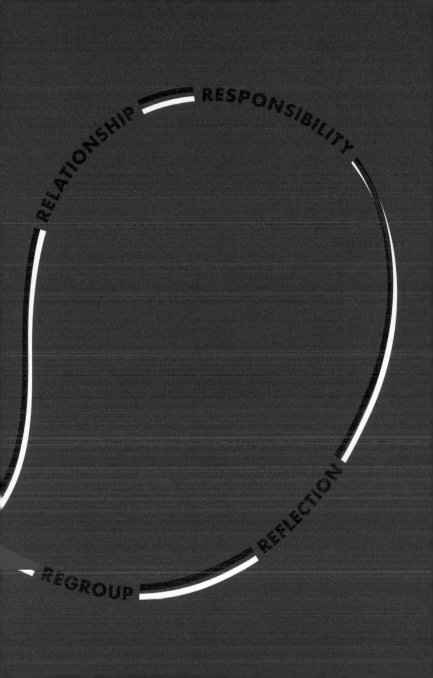

RED

Red is the color of blood, love, life, and passion; of stop signs, bank overdrafts, and scandals. It is confidence, power, and affirmation. Red brings luck and protection.

RITUALS

Celebrating rituals adds attention and intention to the simplest daily tasks.

We all eat, work, love, sleep. What makes us different is how we do it. *See* BATH, BED, DAILY PRACTICES, TABLE.

RELEVANT

To be relevant is to be right and correct for the moment, to be in fashion and in tune with the zeitgeist. The truest barometer for relevance is truth, honesty, and *owning it*— even though it may not always feel like it at the time.

RELATIONSHIP

The most important relationship is the one we have with ourselves. Once we have that, every other relationship is a *PLUS* and not a *MUST*.

RESPONSIBILITY

Contrary to common use of the word, taking responsibility is the key to freedom. *See* FREEDOM, LIBERATED.

REFLECTION

Reflection is taking time to analyze and learn.

Just like a bounce-back of an image through light,
it mirrors to us what we need to know. *See* MIRROR.

REGROUP

To regroup within ourselves is a way to meditate.
See SOLITUDE.

ROUTINE

There is something reassuring about doing the
same things at the same time.

Routine is discipline, habit, and comfort.
See DISCIPLINE, RITUALS.

REGRET

We only regret the things we don't do.

RESTRICTIONS

We hate restrictions, and yet they are often the tools
for creativity and success. *See* CREATIVITY.

WE ALL EAT, WORK, LOVE, SLEEP.

WHAT MAKES US DIFFERENT IS HOW WE DO IT.

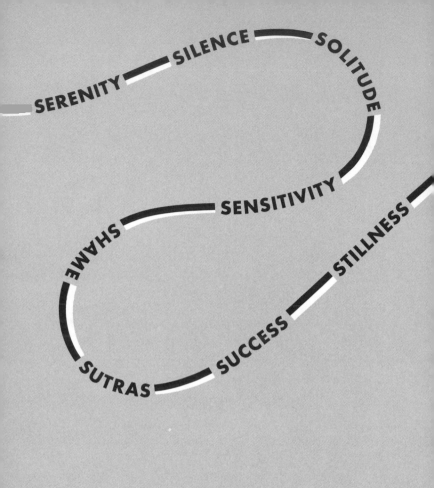

SERENITY — SILENCE — SOLITUDE — SENSITIVITY — SHAME — STILLNESS — SUCCESS — SUTRAS

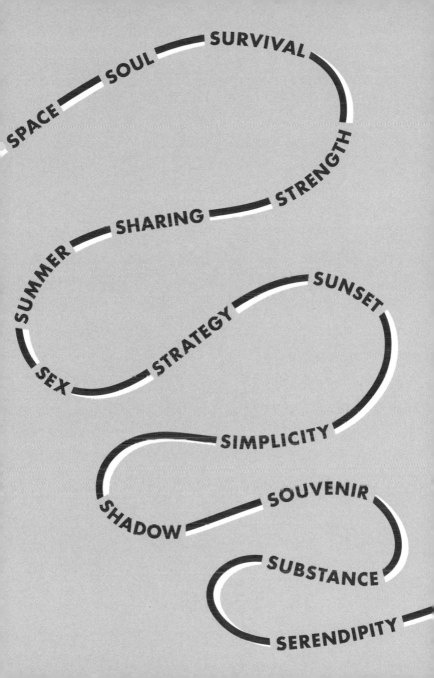

SERENITY

Serenity is an oasis within us. It is about finding ourselves through solitude and silence and owning it. *See* ZEN.

SILENCE

I love silence. I remember an assignment I had at school when I must have been about ten or eleven years old. We were asked to write an essay on our favorite piece of music. I filled an entire page on the beauty of silence. I think my teacher failed me, but I felt proud of my conviction—still am!

SOLITUDE

Solitude is the best place to find strength. Even in a crowd, we sometimes need a moment of solitude to regroup and not lose ourselves. *See* ALONE, REGROUP.

SENSITIVITY

Sensitivity is owning our feelings, not our feelings owning us.

SHAME

Shame must be avoided at all costs. Although it can be hard, when we accept ourselves and our actions, we have no reason to have shame.

SUTRAS

In Sanskrit, *sutra* means an aphorism or a rule; it also means a ribbon that links things together. Deepak Chopra taught me certain *sutras* to affirm and to practice. Sutras for Peace, Harmony, Laughter, Love, Creativity, Affluence, Abundance, Integration, Truth, Freedom, Knowledge, Infinity, Immortality, Enlightenment, and Wholeness.

On my long swims, I practice thankfulness and my gratitude becomes a prayer. I thank God for the protection of all the people who are meaningful in my life and channel their happiness. I pray for them to be who they want to be.

SUCCESS

Success is the achievement of what we want: a dream, a purpose, a goal. For me, when I was growing up, being successful meant being able to be an independent woman leading a man's life—in a woman's body. Although, I apologize if this sounds sexist!

STILLNESS

Stillness is another way to refuel, to find strength and power.

SPACE

Space is true luxury—a luxury we mostly find in nature.

SOUL
Our soul is the invisible energy that is the essence of us. It is our innermost companion guiding us to be good and make good.

SURVIVAL
Survival is the state of being, of existing, of having lived in spite of danger. It is a victory, an assessment of gratitude and humility.

STRENGTH
Strength is the ability to show great physical or mental power, a concentration of energy. Admitting and owning our weaknesses can create strength. *See* ENERGY, POWER.

SHARING
Sharing is loving. It is to offer others what we have, what we feel, and what we have experienced. What we share grows.

SUMMER
Summer is the time when everything is growing, when nature shows off its beauty and its richness. It tastes and smells like a ripe, delicious peach!

SEX

Definitions of male, female, and everything in between, as well as the act of love and reproduction. It seems to be more obsessive for men than women—although that seems sexist for me to say!

STRATEGY

Strategy is a plan of action to execute ideas. In order to make our dreams come true, we must be able to visualize them and build the path. *See* DREAM.

SUNSET

Like autumn is to the year, sunset is to the day. It is the time when the sun goes down and the light shows off its most brilliant colors—a time for reflection and gratitude.

SOUVENIR

Souvenirs are happy past and present moments that create nostalgia and live in our heart as colorful movies. Difficult moments that started with defeat and frustrations can become our most cherished souvenirs because, looking back, they were the seeds for success and have transformed into our most amusing and meaningful anecdotes. *See* PAST.

SIMPLICITY

Simplicity is bringing everything to essential. It is the act of making things easy—a good cleansing process.

SHADOW

Smiling at our own shadow is a sign that we approve who we are.

SUBSTANCE

Substance is the physical material of which something or someone is made. To have substance is standing for something tangible and meaningful. It is the greatest compliment—own it!

SERENDIPITY

Long ago I traveled Sri Lanka by car with a friend who was scouting locations for a movie. We had a wonderful time visiting this magical island with the richest and the most fertile soil where everything grows. Plantations of tea, coffee, peppers, and endless types of fruits delight the sight and surprise visitors at every curve. Before its previous name Ceylon, the island was called *Serendip*—thus the origin of the word *serendipity*, meaning unexpected, beautiful surprises.

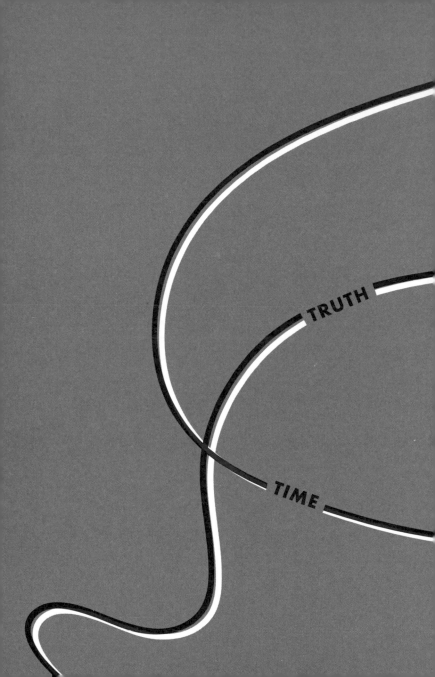

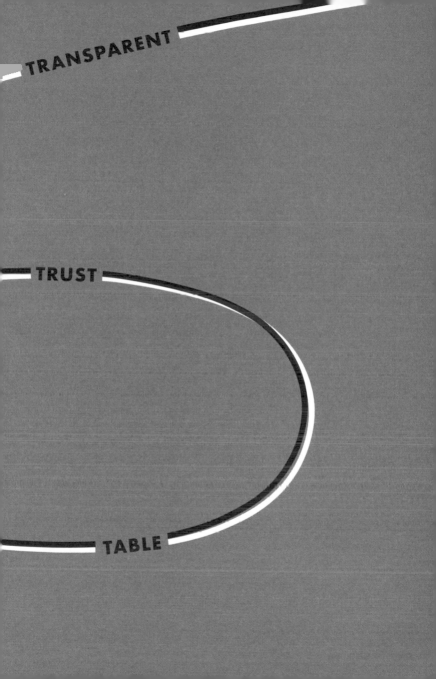

TRANSPARENT

TRUST

TABLE

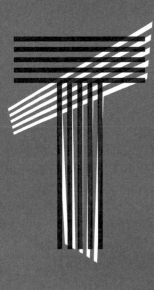

TRUTH

Truth is the quality of embracing reality at all costs—
the most valuable pursuit. Truth is important not only
for what it reveals but for accepting it. The best way to
navigate through life is to practice truth. It is not always
easy, but it is the only way! Accepting the truth keeps
a clean canvas for future plans.

TRUST

The most important person to trust is ourselves. To do that,
we have to surrender to the truth of who we are and what
we can be counted on to do. Trusting others is treating
them as if they are us, until proven to the contrary.

TABLE

Other than the bed, the table is a major place of ritual and
a most important piece of furniture. It is where we eat, where
the family meets, where we assemble and communicate.
A small table, whether in a restaurant or home, can be
where intimacy is created, love is born, and engagements
are decided. "Around the table" and "a seat at the table"
are expressions we use all the time to inspire dialogue
and find solutions.

For me, a very large table is my universe. It is where
I lay my work, the books I need, the white sheets of paper,
and my favorite coloring pencils. Around the table I pace,
I procrastinate, incubate, create. *See* RITUALS.

TIME

"Once upon a time . . ." "What time is it?" "Time to go."
Time is a word we use on a daily basis without paying
attention to its powerful meaning. It measures everything
and cannot be retained. It stretches from eternity to the
furthest future.

True wisdom is knowing the value of time.

TRANSPARENT

To be transparent is having nothing to hide . . .
It is owning it.

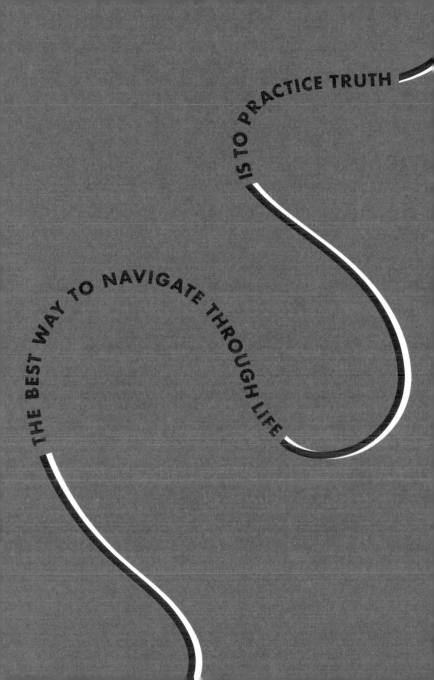

THE BEST WAY TO NAVIGATE THROUGH LIFE IS TO PRACTICE TRUTH

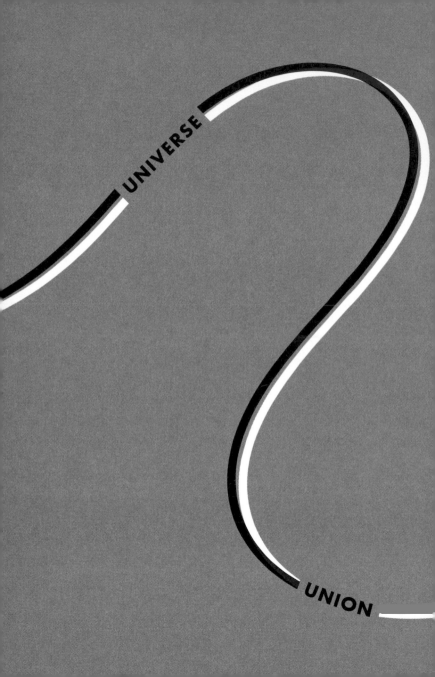

UNIVERSE

UNION

UNITY

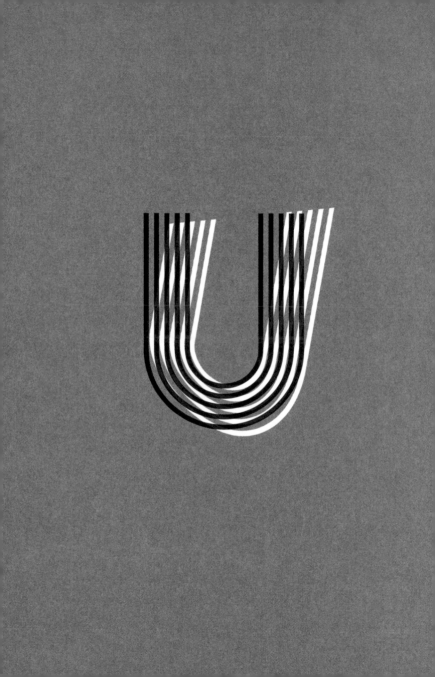

UNIVERSE

Thirteen billion years ago, there was the Big Bang. The universe has been expanding ever since, beyond anything we can ever imagine. It allows us to expand our imagination and our dreams without limitations. To me, nothing is more reassuring than the magnitude of the universe. *See* GEO.

UNION

A union is when two or more people or things blend and become one. Not one getting lost in another, but two fully realized in a perfect alignment.

UNITY

Unity is being in harmony and agreeing. It is the welcome opposite of being divided. *See* HARMONY.

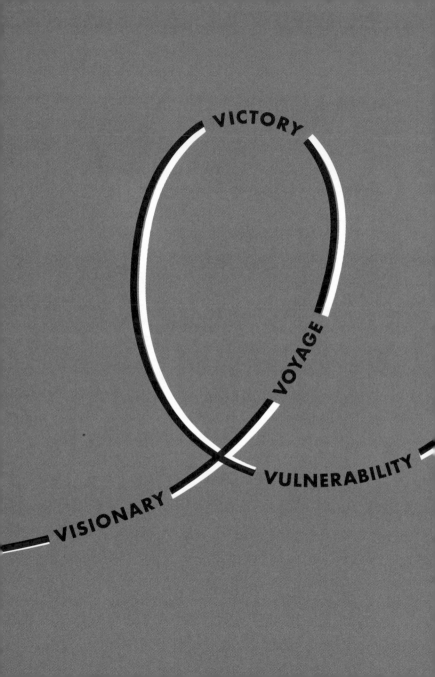

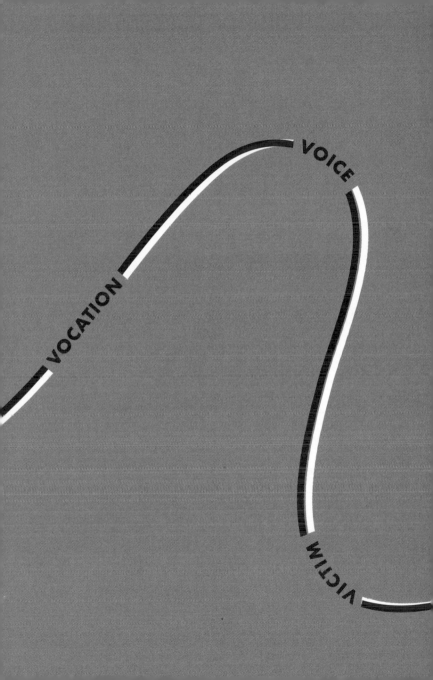

VOICE

VOCATION

VICTIM

VISIONARY

To be a visionary is being able to imagine the future and materialize it. It is daring to dream . . . owning it!

VOYAGE

The French word for journey.

Our longest one is life itself . . . it needs to be enjoyed.
See JOURNEY.

VICTORY

Victory is the total fulfillment of winning a competition or defeating an enemy. Yet the best victories are the silent ones inside ourselves when we conquer our darkness.
See DARKNESS.

VULNERABILITY

When we understand that our vulnerability is an asset, an inspiration to others, and a source of strength, everything changes. No longer a negative, vulnerability becomes a positive.

VOCATION

Not everyone has a vocation from childhood, not everyone has a calling. But if we do, it is a privilege, a necessity that we must pursue at all costs. *See* WORK.

VOICE

There is nothing I admire more than someone who can sing. Not in my case—my parents used to make me sing so that they could laugh.

However, we don't need to sing to have a voice. Being successful at a young age gave me a voice, and gradually I understood the effect of using it. Using my voice, my knowledge, my experiences, and my connections to help others is the best gift I could have asked for.

VICTIM

Not feeling like a victim is our key to courage, strength, and freedom. It is the best lesson and gift my mother ever gave me. *See* WHY ME?

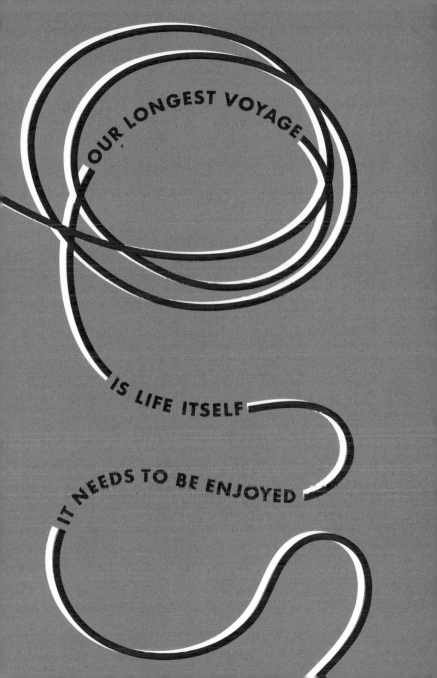

OUR LONGEST VOYAGE

IS LIFE ITSELF

IT NEEDS TO BE ENJOYED

WHITE WORDS WORK

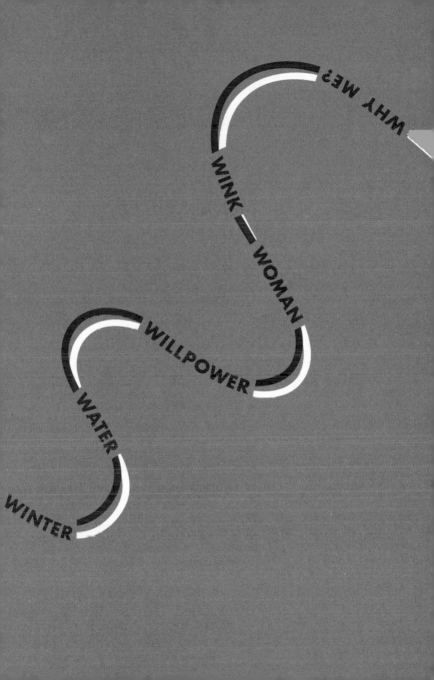

WHY ME?

WINK

WOMAN

WILLPOWER

WATER

WINTER

WHITE

A blank, white paper or canvas is a starting point,
a beginning. A white flag asks for peace.

WORDS

Letters make words, words make sentences. Words are
manifestations of thoughts. Powerful, they carry energy
and need to be used carefully.

To pay attention to words is to pay attention to our
life, our destiny. *See* DESTINY.

WORK

To work is to engage in a mental or physical activity for the
purpose of earning a living or fulfilling a vocation. Work
often becomes our identity, our reason to be. *See* VOCATION.

WINTER

Winter is the last season of the year. No more leaves on
the trees, it is cold; animals hibernate, get inside, sleep,
wait for renewal and for spring. I was born in the winter
on the last day of the year . . . New Year's Eve, December 31.
For me, when the year is over, it is really over—a very
clean cut. That day, I finish a diary and start a fresh one
on January 1, with new resolutions on new blank, white
pages. It is orderly, a ritual that punctuates the year, and
I love it.

WATER

Is there anything more vital than this transparent, odorless liquid that falls from the sky, fills the oceans, seas, and rivers?

There is no life without water, and all living species are made mostly of water. Water is a symbol of purification and healing.

WILLPOWER

To have willpower is to use our own energy to its fullest potential and make things happen.

WOMAN

We all look at the woman across the room with admiration—at work, in a public place, at a party. She looks so composed, secure, and confident. But it is important to know and remember that to her, each one of us is the woman across the room.

WINK

Winking at ourselves and smiling at our shadow are signs of complicity and friendship with ourselves. It means we like and rely on us. *See* SHADOW.

WHY ME?

During my treatment for cancer, one of the nurses said to me, "You're a good patient."

"Why?" I asked.

She explained that there were two categories of patients: the people who ask, "Why me?" and surrender, and the ones who say, "OK, it's happening to me," acknowledge it, and take charge of what they can do, refusing to be victims.

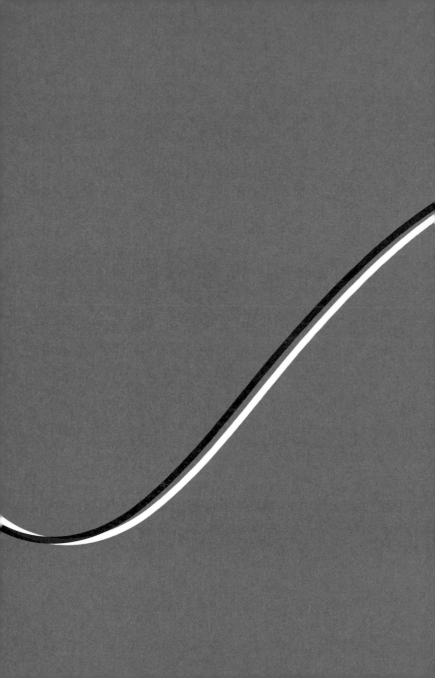

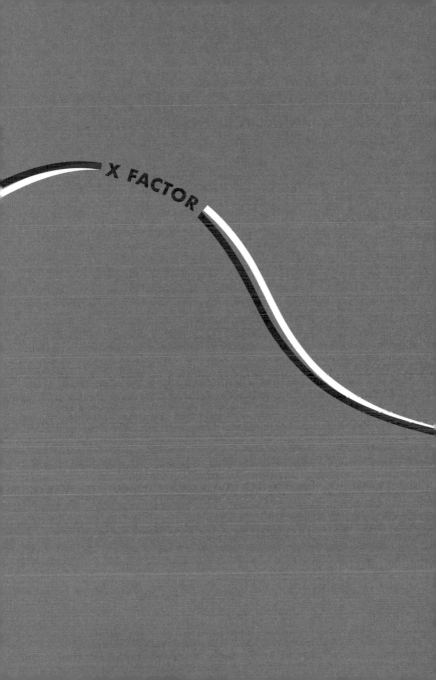
X FACTOR

X FACTOR

In algebra, X is a major symbol attributed to a value to be defined or calculated. Mysterious, it represents a number or a person not stated yet. An X factor is a quality, a special value that can impact and change any given situation. X is also a kiss at the end of a friendly note.

But X will, for me, always be associated with Gustave Eiffel, the architect, engineer, and genius who gave us his famous Parisian tower.

When I was producing the documentary about the Statue of Liberty, *Lady Liberty, Mother of Exiles*, I interviewed the descendants of Eiffel, as he designed the inner structure of the statue, and they explained to me that the genius of Eiffel was the X. His most prolific invention was to discover that emptiness is more resistant to wind than something solid. The wind can pass through. Be it the Eiffel Tower or any bridge or, for that matter, the skeleton of the Statue of Liberty, any construction with an X formation is the most resistant.

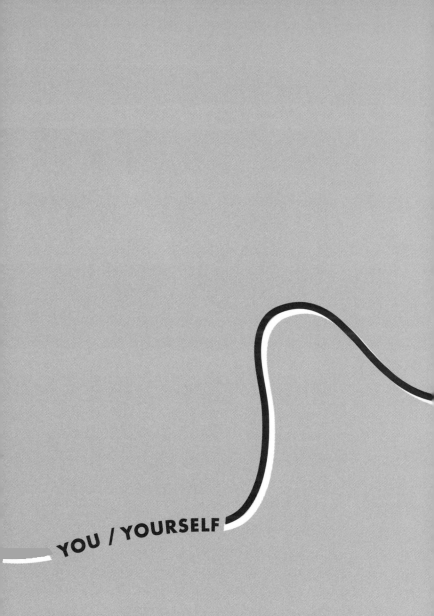

YOU / YOURSELF

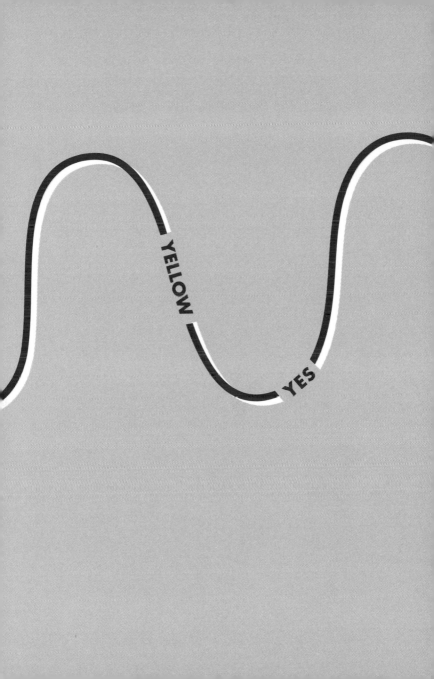

YOU/YOURSELF

You and *yourself* are the two words that I kept wanting to use in this book, and yet each time I did, it felt patronizing. So I used *we* or *ourselves* instead, and it felt right. Anything to learn from this? Maybe to remind ourselves that being part of others makes us more understanding, inclusive, and helpful? Loving ourselves yet being demanding on ourselves is the best way to remind others to do the same.

YELLOW

Between green and orange, the color yellow is explosive and can be seen from afar. It is the color of the sun and of light; of yolk, lemon, and sunflower.

YES

Yes is an expression for positivity, decision, action. *YES, I AM* is the definition of owning it.

"Say. . . yes to life, even in its strangest and harshest problems." —Friedrich Nietzsche

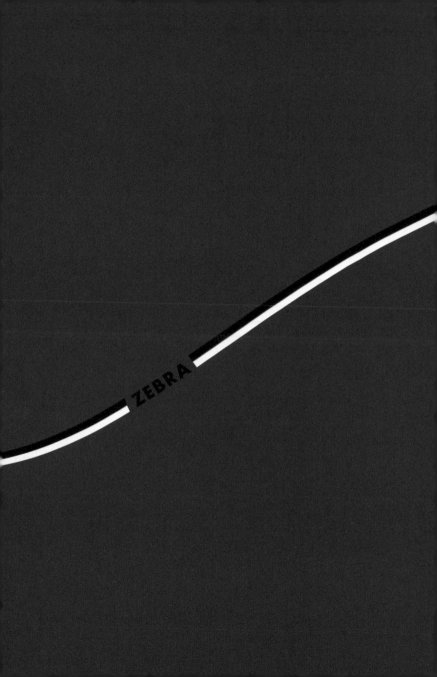

ZEBRA

A zebra is like the most charming small horse, wrapped in a DVF print! I have always loved and used zebra prints in all color ways for clothes, rugs, and home décor.

I remember walking into the glamorous office of Diana Vreeland, the grande dame of fashion and editor in chief of *Vogue* in the early 1970s, and seeing her colored pencils displayed in an empty zebra-motif box that the first pine-scented Rigaud candles came in. It felt like the essence of chic.

ZIGZAG

Zig and *zag* are two words that each mean a sharp turn or a change of direction. Together *zigzag* is a line that moves from left to right and creates endless inspiration for prints . . . it also means going back and forth on a path.

ZEN

Zen is a school of Buddhism that originated in China during the Tang dynasty. It focuses on meditation and breathing. It is also reflected in art, painting, calligraphy, and gardens.

To be Zen is to be fully serene and owning it.
See SERENITY.

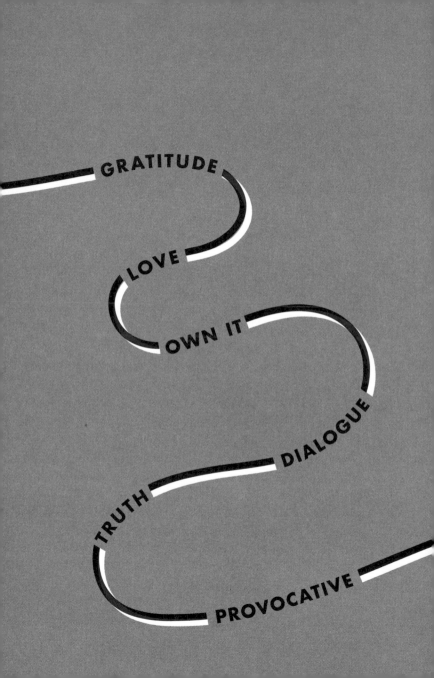

GRATITUDE

LOVE

OWN IT

DIALOGUE

TRUTH

PROVOCATIVE

I want to thank my mother, Lily, for her courage, strength, and inspiration.

My daughter, Tatiana, and granddaughters, Antonia and Talita, for their intelligent criticism and ideas.

Koreen, for her expertise.

François-Marie for the words *assumes toi*.

Sarah, Edward, Alec, Jane, Kate, Martine, Brittan, Isaac, and Sam for their suggestions.

The Phaidon team: Billy, for coming up with the idea; Keith and Deborah, for accepting it; Lynne, for her incredible patience; Hans, for his beautiful design inspired by the sutras.

Phaidon Press Limited
2 Cooperage Yard
London E15 2QR

Phaidon Press Inc.
65 Bleecker Street
New York, NY 10012

phaidon.com

First published 2021
Reprinted 2021
© 2021 by Diane von Fürstenberg

ISBN 978 1 83866 222 6
ISBN 978 1 83866 232 5 (Signed edition)

A CIP catalogue record for this book
is available from the British Library and
the Library of Congress.

Commissioning Editor: William Norwich
Project Editor: Lynne Ciccaglione
Production Controller: Lily Rodgers
Cover Concept: YummyColours
Cover and Interior Design: Hans Stofregen

Printed in the USA